THE CHURCH: ICON
of the
TRINITY
A Brief Study

Bruno Forte

Translated by Robert Paolucci

St. Paul Books & Media

Nihil Obstat:
   Rev. Paul E. Ritt, S.T.D.

Imprimatur:
   +Bernard Cardinal Law
   June 25, 1991

Library of Congress Cataloging-in-Publication Data

Forte, Bruno.
   [La Chiesa icona della Trinita. English]
   The Church, icon of the Trinity : a brief study of the Church /
   Bruno Forte ; translated by Robert Paolucci.
         p.   cm.
   Translation of: La Chiesa icona della Trinita.
   Includes bibliographical references.
   ISBN 0-8198-1482-2 (pbk.)
   1. Church.   I. Title.
BX1746.F6713   1991   91-27889
262'.7 — dc20   CIP

Printed and published in the U.S.A. by St. Paul Books & Media
50 St. Paul's Ave., Boston MA 02130

St. Paul Books & Media is the publishing house of the Daughters of
St. Paul, an international congregation of women religious serving the
Church with the communications media.

1 2 3 4 5 6 7 8 9   98 97 96 95 94 93 92 91

Contents

Preface 7

I. The Church From the Trinity:
Ecclesia de Trinitate 9

Where Does the Church Come from? 9

  1. The Trinitarian Origin of the Church 12
    1.1 The Renewal of Ecclesiology 12
    1.2 The Council of the Church 18
    1.3 The Trinitarian Ecclesiology of Vatican II 22

II. The Church Between Times:
Ecclesia Inter Tempora 33

What Is the Church? The Trinitarian Form
of the Church 33

  2. The Church as People of God 38
    2.1 People of God: Community, Charisms
       and Ministries 38
    2.2 People of God and Laicity of the
       Whole Church 50

  3. The Church as Communion 62
    3.1 The Ecclesiology of Communion 62
    3.2 The "Priority" of the Local Church
       in the Ecclesiology of Communion 68
    3.3 The Communion of Churches 77

III. The Pilgrim Church:
   Ecclesia Viatorum 85

Where Is the Church Heading? 85

   4. The Trinitarian Goal of the Church 88
       4.1 The Eschatological Nature of
           the Pilgrim Church 88
       4.2 On the Way to a Fuller Unity 95

Notes 105

Preface

For the first time, after thirty years of serving the cause of unity, the Ecumenical Institute of Bossey (Switzerland), affiliated with the World Council of Churches, associated with the University of Geneva, organized a seminar on Roman Catholicism. The purpose of the seminar — a joint effort with the Secretariat for Promoting Christian Unity and held between May 10 and 20, 1983 — was to present the various aspects of the Catholic Church to theologians and pastors of different Christian faiths from all over the world. To that end, I was asked to give a lecture on how the Catholic Church sees itself since Vatican Council II. That gave birth to these readings which, taken as a whole, form a "brief study on the Church" keyed to three basic questions: Where does the Church come from? What is the Church? Where is the Church heading?

Tested out in the ecumenical reception they received at Bossey, these reflections, though not exhaustive, may be of help to the person who — whether Catholic or not — wishes to understand better the self-awareness of the churches in communion with Rome, in view of the growth in unity which Christ wants.

In obedience to this will of the Lord, the following pages have been conceived and written. May he make them useful and fruitful, well beyond their limitations.

Bruno Forte
Feast of Pentecost, 1983

First Part

The Church From the Trinity:
Ecclesia de Trinitate

Where Does the Church Come From?

Before Vatican Council II, the prevailing view of the Church in Catholic theology was characterized by what Yves Congar described as "Christomonism." The term denotes the special attention given to the visible, "incarnationist" aspects of the Church. This view downplays the mystery-sacrament dimension, whereby what is visible is an evocation, sign and instrument of a fuller and more life-giving invisible reality.

The first chapter of the Constitution on the Church *(Lumen Gentium)* describes the restoration of the

Trinitarian depth of the Church: "A people made one with the unity of the Father, the Son and the Holy Spirit" (St. Cyprian), the Church comes from the Trinity, is structured in the image of the Trinity, and journeys toward the Trinitarian fulfillment of history. Coming from on high ("oriens ex alto": "dayspring from on high"), molded from on high and on her journey to the height ("Regnum Dei praesens in mysterio": "the Kingdom of Christ now present in mystery," LG 3), the Church cannot be reduced to the mere coordinates of history, of what is visible and at our disposal.

The Church comes from the Trinity: the Father's universal saving plan (LG 2), the Son's mission (LG 3), and the Holy Spirit's sanctifying work (LG 4) establish the Church as a "mystery," a divine work in our human time, prepared from the very beginning ("Ecclesia ab Abel": "the Church from Abel"), gathered by the Incarnate Word ("Ecclesia creatura Verbi": "the Church, creature of the Word"), always vivified anew by the Holy Spirit (the Church, the "temple of the Holy Spirit").

The Church is the icon of the Holy Trinity: by "no weak analogy," she is compared to the mystery of the Incarnate Word (LG 8), in the dialectic of what is visible and invisible. At the same time, her "communion," her oneness in the variety of local churches and charisms and ministries therein, reflects the Trinitarian communion (cf. Chapters II-VI of *Lumen Gentium*).

The Church is journeying toward the Trinity. It is

a Church of pilgrims in which, through perennial change and reform ("Ecclesia semper reformanda": "the Church always in need of being purified"), in communion with the heavenly Church, its final glory is already being prepared (cf. Chapters VII and VIII of *Lumen Gentium*).

1. The Trinitarian Origin of the Church

1.1 The Renewal of Ecclesiology

The prevailing view of the Church in Catholic theology before Vatican II was characterized by what Yves Congar called "Christomonism."[1] This expression indicates the special attention given to the Christological aspects of the Church and, hence, to her visible and institutional dimension. This accentuation developed in medieval ecclesiology in relation, on the one hand, to the historical-political role that the Christian community was assuming especially in its hierarchical components; and, on the other hand, to the separation introduced into the mystery, by clearly distinguishing between the "true" Body of Christ in the Eucharist, and the Church understood as the mystical Body of Christ, in reaction to the "new" doctrines introduced into eucharistic theology (by Berengario and others).

This tendency came to a head in the ecclesiology of the Counter Reformation. It laid full stress on the visible and institutional manifestations of the ecclesial community, as the alternative to a presumed "invisibilism" advocated by the Reformers. In the systematic teaching of Robert Bellarmine, the Church "is the community of people gathered together through profession of the true faith, the reception of the same sacraments and under the governance of the legitimate pastors and, in particular, the sole Vicar of Christ on earth, the Roman Pontiff [...]. We believe that to be considered a member of this true Church, of which the Scriptures speak, one need not have any interior virtue. All that is needed is an exterior profession of the Faith and of the communion of sacraments — things which the senses themselves can ascertain [...]. The Church, in fact, is a community of men and women as visible and palpable as the community of the Roman people, or the Kingdom of France, or the Republic of Venice."[2]

The main feature of this definition is an insistence on visibility, conceived in a pyramidal form: the "totality" that the Church is, united by one Faith and by the same sacraments, is seen as comprising parts or portions, interconnected and rising to a summit under the leadership of the visible Head of the Church community: the Bishop of Rome. The local bishops are seen as representatives of the Universal Pastor, to the point that the doctrine of the sacramental nature of the episcopacy was rejected by many, because it seemed to involve a simple delegation of powers, conferred by the top echelon of the Church's hierarchical structure. This view, however, is the extreme fruit of a number of consecutive reactions. Against regalism, which tended to subordinate spiritual power to temporal power, there developed a theology of hierarchical powers and of the Church as an organized kingdom (e.g., Egidius Romanus). Against conciliar theories, which subordinated the ministry of the Pope to the authority of the Council, the role of the papal primacy was emphasized. Against the spiritualism of Wycliffe and Hus, the ecclesiastical and social dimensions of Christianity were pointed up: against the Reformation, there was a desire to reaffirm the objective value of the means of grace, particularly of the sacraments and the hierarchical ministry. Even after the systematizing done by Bellarmine, the visibilist and juridical conception of the Church was further stressed in the face of new reactions; against Jansenism, more or less linked to episcopal and regalist Gallicanism, which tended to emphasize the role of the national churches, the powers of Roman centralism were reaffirmed; against the secularism and state absolutism of the nineteenth century, the Church was highlighted as a perfect society ("societas perfecta"), endowed with her own sufficient rights and means; against Modernism, lastly, there was a vigorous affirmation of the prerogatives of the teaching Church. Without denying the presence of prophetic voices such as those of J. A. Moehler, A. Rosmini and of the nineteenth century Roman School, bent on rediscovering the Church in her interior nature and her mystery, we can say that the development of Catholic ecclesiology on the threshold of the twentieth century was more the fruit of reactions and defensiveness than the joyful and liberating announcement of the "mystery," hidden for centuries and revealed in Christ. The need for a renewal in ecclesiology was therefore connected to the limitations of the theology of the manuals and the schools. There was an awareness of the need for a rethinking which, reaching back to the sources of the Faith, would unfold the richness of its horizons. There was an awareness, also in ecclesiology, that beyond the "letter" there is need for the life-giving and liberating presence of the Holy Spirit....

The "century of the Church" — as we have heard the twentieth century called[3] — was ushered in already marked by this need: the crisis provoked by the First World War only brought it out. The collapse of trust in different institutions, the sufferings experienced and the new desire for an interior life, spurred people on to a rebirth of social awareness (the development of sociological studies, international society, and so forth), at the same time reawakening in them a religious yearning. The most profound and impelling causes of renewal in ecclesiology, however, were of a spiritual origin. They are to be seen in the vigorous awareness of the supernatural stirred up by anti-Modernist action, in the liturgical movement, in the intensifying of eucharistic life, in the return to biblical and patristic sources, in the rediscovery of the laity's active role, in the early impulses of the modern ecumenical movement — in short, in a "spiritual enthusiasm which was *lived* before being formulated."[4]

The new view of the Church is seen as an overcoming of the visibilist and juridical conception of the Counter Reformation, in the sense of a "rediscovery of the Church's supernatural and mystical elements, of a humble and religious attempt to consider in all its divine depth the *mystery of the Church.*"[5] The renewal — focusing especially on the theology of the Fathers and of Scholasticism — restores the pneumatological and Christological dimensions of ecclesial reality. The theology of the Church as the Mystical Body of Christ buds forth and develops with inspiring force.[6]

Exaggerations, resistance and defensiveness arose that led to the intervention of papal teaching. The encyclical *Mystici Corporis* (June 29, 1943) would offset the risk entailed in an ecclesiology of the Mystical Body, i.e., that of reducing the Church to a purely interior experience, by affirming the equation between the Mystical Body and the Roman Catholic Church. But while the encyclical thus confirms the triumph of the idea, it also indicates its limits thus concluding the first stages of renewal of ecclesiology and unwittingly opening the way to further developments.

The Second World War shed light in an even more striking way on the crisis of the First War. In addition, it stepped up technological and industrial advances, in efforts toward postwar reconstruction. But it thereby widened the distance between the economically healthy countries and the so-called Third World. Never before as in those years was there awareness of the malaise of the Church-world relationship in face of the enormous growth of the "secular city" and the problems of development and hunger. History was making dramatic inquiries of the Church.

In terms of ecclesiological reflection, now that the mystery of the Church's interior life in Christ and in the Holy Spirit was rediscovered, we were faced with the problem of rethinking the Church community as an historical reality. This aspect had been partly overlooked since the early days of the renewal, which were marked by a reaction to the excessive visibilism of the past. This "historical" approach to the mystery of the Church was stimulated also by the flowering of biblical studies, proper to this period, and by the partly new method for studying the Fathers, based on reading their works and ideas in their original historical context. History thus came to question the Church not only on her manifestation to the world but also on her own self-reflection.

Emerging under the impetus of this "challenge" were concepts of the Church as a "sacrament," as the "People of God," as a "communion" or fellowship of people and churches. Vatican Council II took up these ideas, rejecting any reduction of the Church community to a single spiritual reality or a single visible reality. It put forward the Church's "mystery" of communion flowing from the Trinity and having the Trinity as a goal. The Church is a people en route between the "already" of Christ's first coming, which has brought them together, and the "not yet" of his return, which permeates them with a committed and joyful hope.

1.2   The Council of the Church

Vatican II was characterized from the outset as the Council of the Church: "Let the Council be a Council 'about the Church' and be divided into two parts: *"de Ecclesia ad intra – de Ecclesia ad extra": "the Church looking within itself – the Church looking outward."*[7] "What is the Church? What does the Church do? These questions are like two keystones around which all the questions of this Council must fit into place."[8]

The architecture of the Council is thus simple and solid: the two pillars of that architecture are the Dogmatic Constitution on the Church *(Lumen Gentium)* and the Pastoral Constitution on the Church in the Modern World *(Gaudium et Spes)*. The former looks at the Church in itself, exploring its mystery; the latter considers the role of the Church in the world. The other documents of the Council serve only to express and explore what is treated in these two constitutions in the organic unity of an overall view.

The entire message of the Council is thus permeated by an ecclesiological reflection. The Council takes up the concerns of the renewal of the Church's awareness of itself and of its mission in history. A Council of the Church, it has been a Church event, an experience of communion and thanksgiving (the

Council is *celebrated!)* In that experience, under the action of the Holy Spirit, the Church was wholly intent upon God's Word in order to rediscover herself in the face of the expectations of the people of our day. Faithful to her God and faithful to history, the Church in Council wanted to couple these fidelities, in the school of the One who is in person the focal point of the two worlds, the present world and the world to come: Jesus Christ, her Lord, the light of nations.

This intention is clearly expressed from the very first words of the *Constitution on the Church.* They express the threefold concern about fidelity to her own identity which comes from Christ (the Christological perspective), fidelity to humankind, which the Church is to serve (anthropological perspective), and the encounter of both fidelities, in the mystery of a covenant, which is the Church (sacramental perspective): "Christ is the Light of nations. Because this is so, this Sacred Synod, gathered together in the Holy Spirit, eagerly desires, by proclaiming the Gospel to every creature (cf. Mk 16:15), to bring the light of Christ to all people, a light brightly visible on the countenance of the Church [Christological perspective]. Since the Church is in Christ like a sacrament or as a sign and instrument both of a very closely knit union with God and of the unity of the whole human race, it desires now to unfold more fully to the faithful of the Church and to the whole world its own inner nature and universal mission. This it intends to do following faithfully the teaching of previous councils [sacramental perspective]. The present-day conditions of the world add greater urgency to this work of the Church so that all people, joined more closely today by various social, technical and cultural ties, might also attain fuller unity in Christ [anthropological perspective]" (LG 1).

The profound connection between the three perspectives, as brought out by the text, shows that the Church's faithfulness to her identity in Christ and preoccupation with her historical relevance in the service of humankind are not alternatives nor are they separable. For they belong together in a Church which, to be the saving presence of her Lord among his people, must be a place of covenant *(foederis arca),* totally faithful to heaven and at the same time totally faithful to the earth, totally of Christ and at the same time totally for humankind.

This encounter of the two imperative fidelities calls for the supplanting of any ecclesiological reductionism: either of the secular type, which makes the Church one actor among the various actors in history with consideration given only to her visible historical impact; or of the spiritualistic type, which exalts the invisible dimension of the Church to the detriment of her concrete human reality. The Council has kept its distance from this twofold, possible reductionism.

From the very beginning, the Church has presented herself as a "mystery": this is the biblical-Pauline idea of the divine plan of salvation being worked out in time upon earth, of the Glory already hidden and at work in the signs of history. The Church offers herself as the place of encounter between divine initiative and human activity, the presence of the Trinity in time and in a certain sense, of time in the Trinity, irreducible to a purely human Church and yet a Church of people living fully in history. The visibilist-juridical, barren quality of the preparatory draft document, which opened with a chapter on the nature of the Church Militant, placed the terms "Church society," "Roman Catholic Church" and "Mystical Body of Christ," on an equal level. It expounded on the members of the Church Militant and the Church's authority, obedience and relations with the outside world.[9] This treatment was replaced by the restoration of the Trinitarian depth of ecclesial reality, but without losing sight of its historical building-blocks. Chapter I of *Lumen Gentium,* "De Ecclesiae Mysterio" (the Mystery of the Church), shows at once that the Council took its insistent cue both from the beginning of Church renewal of the twentieth century, concerned with regaining the Church's interior and supernatural dimension, and from the developments of that renewal, keyed to reading in history the fruit of Trinitarian initiative, i.e., ecclesial communion.

In the ecclesial "mystery" not only is the emphasis on the visible that characterized the Counter Reformation surmounted but also the historical dimension of the Church "between times" is restored: the Church, that is to say, between its origin in the divine mission and its fulfillment in the glory of God, who is all in all. The Council of the Church thus restores to Catholic ecclesiology, at the same time, the freshness and

depth of its relationship to the Trinity and the awareness of an existence, a presence in history that is not
simply a part of history.

1.3   The Trinitarian Ecclesiology
of Vatican II

The key to understanding the Council's ecclesiological message, geared to surmounting any form of
reductionism so as to have a renewed and full perception of the mystery of the Church, lies in a Trinitarian
perspective of the Church: "De unitate Patris et Filii
et Spiritus Sancti plebs adunata": "a people made one
with the unity of the Father, the Son and the Holy
Spirit."[10] The Church, as presented in Chapter I of
Lumen Gentium, comes from the Trinity. She is
structured in the image of the Trinity and journeys
toward the Trinitarian fulfillment of history. Dawn-
ing upon us from on high ("oriens ex alto") like her
Lord (Lk 1:78), molded from on high and on the road
leading on high, for she is the "kingdom of Christ now
present in mystery" (LG 3), the Church is in history.
And yet, she is not reducible to the dimensions of
history, of what is visible and passing.

This basic intuition, which comes from the testimony of Scripture (consider the Pauline theology of
"mystery" and the ordered plan of the divine mission)
and from the faithful reflection of the Fathers of the
Church, is developed throughout the Dogmatic Constitution on the Church (*Lumen Gentium*). This constitution examines in order the origin, the present

reality, and the future of the Church in the light of the Holy Trinity. Where does the Church come from? What is the Church? Where is the Church heading? These are the three basic questions, therefore, that the Council wanted to answer in terms of the origin, the form and the Trinitarian goal of ecclesial communion.

The Trinitarian origin of the Church is presented by describing the ordered plan of salvation. The object of the Father's plan, which is unstinting and inscrutable, i.e., freely given and unfathomable, is to raise his people to participation in the divine life in communion with the Trinity: "The eternal Father, by a free and hidden plan of his own wisdom and goodness, created the whole world. His plan was to raise humankind to a participation of the divine life" (LG 2).

In spite of sin, the Father has brought about this plan in view of Christ and in him, "the first-born of all creation," "the first-born among many brethren," i.e., the center of creation and redemption, brought together in a single plan of salvation (cf. Col 1:15 and Rom 8:29). The unity of human beings with God and among themselves, attained through the reconciling action of the Incarnate Word, is realized historically in the Church and will be brought to fulfillment in glory. "He planned to assemble in the holy Church all those who would believe in Christ. Already from the beginning of the world the foreshadowing of the Church took place. It was prepared in a remarkable way throughout the history of the people of Israel and by means of the Old Covenant. In the present era of time, the Church was constituted and, by the outpouring of the Spirit, was made manifest. At the end of time she will gloriously achieve completion, when, as is read in the holy Fathers, all the just from Adam and 'from Abel, the just one, to the last of the elect' will be gathered together with the Father in the universal Church" (LG 2).

The Church is here understood in a very broad sense – "Ecclesia ab Abel usque ad ultimum electum" ("the Church from Abel to the last of the elect") – according to a universalism of Pauline origin (related to Paul's "cosmic Christology") and very widespread in the thinking of the Fathers. We do not want to deny the necessity of the Church for salvation: we want to affirm that, in her visible and historical form, she is the sacrament, i.e, the sign and chosen instrument, of God's plan of unity, which goes from creation to the "second coming." That is to say, the Church is the historical participation in Trinitarian unity, the embodiment begun under the veil of the signs of salvation springing from the divine initiative, the mystery or sacrament "of a very closely knit union with God and of the unity of the whole human race" (LG 1).

The divine plan of unity took form, in the fullness of time, with the mission and work of the Son. He inaugurated on earth the Kingdom of Heaven. The Church is the presence of that kingdom "in mystery," i.e., the sign and seed that both reveals and hides, growing visibly toward fulfillment through the power of God (cf. LG 3). "This inauguration and this growth are both symbolized by the blood and water which flowed from the open side of the crucified Jesus (cf. Jn 19:34), and are foretold in the words of the Lord referring to his death on the cross: 'And I, if I am lifted up from the earth, will draw all men to myself' (Jn 12:34ff.)" (LG 3).

In the blood and water flowing from the side of Christ crucified, the Fathers have seen the sacraments of Baptism and the Eucharist: the idea is that from Christ, our Passover, derives the Church's sacramental structure. The other text quoted from John (Jn 12:34ff.) indicates the crowning of the sacrifice of the cross: the lifting up, i.e., the glorious Resurrection, the sign of the Father's acceptance of the offering and of the consequent reconciliation of all people with him and with each other. Even as at the center of the Father's plan there is the mission of the Son, to whom the Church is indissolubly joined, at the center of the Son's mission there is his passover mystery, from which the Church is born as the community of those who have been reconciled in Christ to God and to each other.

This mystery is not simply an event of the past. It is made present in the memorial of the Eucharist, to reconcile all people in the here and now of their history. "The Eucharist is the memorial of Christ crucified and risen, i.e., the living and effective sign of his sacrifice, accomplished once and for all on the cross and still operative on behalf of all human-kind."[11]

"As often as the sacrifice of the cross in which

'Christ our Passover, has been sacrificed' (1 Cor 5:7), is celebrated on an altar, the work of our redemption is carried on, and in the sacrament of the Eucharistic bread, the unity of all believers who form one body in Christ (cf. 1 Cor 10:17) is both expressed and brought about. All people are called to this union with Christ, who is the light of the world, from whom we go forth, through whom we live, and toward whom our whole life strains" (LG 3). The Church, which celebrates the Eucharist, comes from the Eucharist as the Body of Christ in history.[12]

The Son's mission culminates in the sending of the Spirit: through Christ, the Spirit makes possible our access to the Father. Just as the Father through the Son comes to us in the Spirit, so too we in the Spirit through the Son can now have access to the Father. The movement of descent makes possible the movement of ascent, in a circuit of unity, whose eternal phase is the Trinity and whose temporal phase is the Church. The Spirit gives life (cf. Jn 4:14; 7:38-39; Rom 8:10-11, quoted by LG 4): the Spirit "dwells in the Church and in the hearts of the faithful as in a temple (cf. 1 Cor 3:16; 6:19). In them he prays on their behalf and bears witness to the fact that they are adopted sons (cf. Gal 4:6; Rom 8:15-16 and 26). The Church, which the Spirit guides in the way of all truth (cf. Jn 16:13) and which he unified in communion and in works of ministry, he both equips and directs with hierarchical and charismatic gifts and adorns with his fruits (cf. Eph 4:11-12; 1 Cor 12:4; Gal 5:22). By the power of the Gospel the Spirit makes the Church keep the freshness of youth, uninterruptedly renews it and leads it to perfect union with its Spouse. The Spirit and the bride both say to the Lord Jesus, 'Come!' (cf. Rev 22:17)" (LG 4).

The Church willed by the Father is therefore the creature of the Son ("creatura Verbi": creature of the Word of God), given new life perennially by the Holy Spirit: she is truly "the work of the Holy Trinity. Even as humankind is made in God's image and divine activity is reflected in human knowledge and love, so the Church who represents Jesus Christ must be the manifestation, in time, of Trinitarian life. There is an epiphany of God the Creator through human beings and there is an epiphany of the One and Triune God through Christ and his Church: 'As the Father has sent me, even so I send you' (Jn 20:21)."[13]

The Church comes from the Trinity. She is the "Ecclesia de Trinitate": "The Latin preposition 'de' evokes both the idea of imitation and that of participation. It is 'from' this unity between divine hypostases that the 'unification' of God's people is prolonged: by becoming united, the latter participate in another Unity; so that for St. Cyprian the Church's unity is no longer intelligible apart from that of the Trinity."[14]

"This communication in unity, accomplished inseparably by the Son and by the Spirit, at work in relation to the Father and his plan, is the Church in her fullness."[15] The Trinitarian perspective of ecclesial communion thus extends throughout the Church's history, from her origin through her present existence and her future. The Trinity is seen as the rich and inexhaustible response not only to the question, "Where is the Church coming from?" but also to those questions about what the Church is and where she is going. This is shown by the way *Lumen Gentium* was developed.

The Church is the icon of the Holy Trinity, i.e., her communion is structured in the image and likeness of the Trinitarian communion. "By no weak analogy, [this reality] is compared to the mystery of the Incarnate Word. As the assumed nature inseparably united to the Divine Word serves as a living organ of salvation, so, in a similar way, does the visible social structure of the Church serve the Spirit of Christ who gives it life, in the building up of the body (cf. Eph 4:16)" (LG 8).

So by analogy the Church can be likened to the divine communion: one in the diversity of Persons, in a fruitful exchange of relations. Just as "in divinis" love is a distinction of Persons and a canceling out of what is distinct in the unity of the mystery, so too in the Church, apart from the infinite distance that separates heaven and earth but also by virtue of the infinite communion established by the Son's Incarnation, love is a "distinction and canceling out (*Aufheben*) of what is distinct" (Hegel). The variety of gifts and services must converge in the unity of God's people, even as the variety of local churches, each one a full embodiment of the Catholic Church in a definite place and time, is called to live and express itself in their reciprocal fellowship. The Church, structured on the example of the Trinity, must keep far from not only a uniformity which degrades and undercuts the originality and richness of the Spirit's gifts, but also from any hurtful conflict which does not resolve in fellowship the tension between different charisms and ministries, in a fruitful and reciprocal acceptance of both persons and communities in the unity of faith, hope and love (cf. Chapters II-IV of LG).

The Trinity, the source and exemplary image of the Church, is the goal of that Church. Born of the Father, through the Son, in the Holy Spirit, the ecclesial communion must return to the Father in the Spirit through the Son, until the day when everything is subject to the Son and he turns over everything to the Father, so that "God may be everything to every one" (1 Cor 15:28).

The Trinity is the origin and destiny toward which the pilgrim people are heading. It is the "already" and the "not yet" of the Church, the prime past and the promised future, the beginning and the end. This final destination in Glory, in which the fellowship of believers will forever be inserted in the fullness of divine life, is the basis of the eschatological nature of the pilgrim Church, which Vatican II has rediscovered and reintroduced into ecclesial awareness. The Church does not possess its fulfillment in this present age, but looks forward to it and prepares for it until the day when her Lord will come again and everything will be perfectly re-established in him. She is therefore always in a state of becoming, never arrived; for that reason, she "must always be re-formed," needful of continual purification and perennial renewal, in the power of the Holy Spirit, who works in the Church so that God's promises may be brought to fulfillment.

Thus, in the season of the "meantime" between Christ's first coming and his glorious return, the Church lives in fidelity to the present world and fidelity to the world to come, overshadowed by the Holy Spirit, like the welcoming Virgin Mary, who is both the member par excellence and the icon of the Church, nurtured by what has been given to her for growth in the long advent of history to become what has not yet been completed in her. The Church "between times" journeys toward the Trinity, by way of invocation, praise and service, under the weight of the contradictions of the present and rich in the glory of the promise (cf. Chapter VII of LG on the eschatological nature of the pilgrim Church and Chapter VIII on the Virgin Mary Mother of God, in the mystery of Christ and the Church). "Inter persecutiones mundi et consolationes Dei peregrinando procurrit Ecclesia"[16]: "like a pilgrim in a foreign land, the Church presses forward amid the persecutions of the world and the consolations of God"; strong in the faithfulness of its God and tested beneath the weight of opposition and rejection, the Church advances on its pilgrimage toward the Trinitarian fulfillment of history.

The Church comes from the Trinity, journeys toward it, and is structured in its image. Everything the Council has said about the Church is summed up in this remembrance or recollection of the origin, the form and Trinitarian goal of ecclesial communion. The barren emphasis on visibility which characterized the past could not be surmounted in a more radical way; fidelity to history could not be expressed with more compelling insistence. The Church of the Council is — in continuity with the witness of Scripture and the Fathers — the Church of the Trinity, the "Ecclesia de Trinitate."

Second Part

The Church Between Times: *Ecclesia Inter Tempora*

What is the Church? The Trinitarian Form of the Church

The Church as People of God

Ecclesiology in the Catholic Church before Vatican II stressed the hierarchical element in the conception and practice of ecclesial life ("hierarchology"). We had reached the point of affirming that "God created this hierarchy and thus provided for the Church's needs until the end of the world." The wealth and variety of the gifts received by believers at baptism and their "universal priesthood," were overshadowed by the teaching, worshiping and pastoral functions proper only to the hierarchical ministry.

In emphasizing anew the Church's Trinitarian foundation, Vatican II has restored also the primacy of "total ecclesiology," i.e., of the unity that precedes distinction and is both its forerunner and its goal. With the chapter on the entire People of God placed before the treatise on the hierarchy, *Lumen Gentium* marks an authentic "Copernican revolution." It points out our baptismal dignity, that anointing proper to the "common priesthood," by virtue of which everyone in the Church participates — though according to different forms and services — in the prophecy, priesthood and kingship of the Lord Jesus. The same hierarchical ministry is thus seen in the Church and through the Church, never outside of her.

Further study in the postconciliar years has developed this renewed aspect in describing the Church "between times" — placed, that is, between the *already* of its Trinitarian origin and the *not yet* of the promised glory — as the completely charismatic and completely ministerial People of God. From the dual concept "hierarchy-laity," which distinguishes too greatly what Baptism unites and at the same time distinguishes too little what the gifts of the Holy Spirit bring about, we have moved on to the dual concept of "community-charisms and ministries," where unity comes before distinction and the gifts and services are seen in that unity and through that unity. The Church is rediscovered as being wholly enriched with numerous charisms and — since a charism is for the service of the community — wholly ministerial. Among the ministries — charisms put to service recognized by the Church — is the *ordained ministry,* linked in the sacrament of Holy Orders, a ministry of unity in representing Christ the Head of the Church Body, indispensable for the life and growth of the community.

The rediscovery of total ecclesiology leads also to accepting "laicity," or the lay state, as a fundamental dimension of the entire Church, in the surmounting of all ecclesiocentrism. In the different inter-church relationships, accepting laicity implies recognizing the dignity proper to each person in the Church; hence, an affirmation of the freedom of the Christian, of the self-determination and shared responsibility of each one in the community (laicity *in* the Church). In terms of the temporal order, the laicity of the Church means ordination to the service and mission inherent in the anthropology of grace and, therefore, the responsibility of every baptized person in the work of mediating between salvation and history. Lastly, acceptance of laicity in ecclesiology implies recognizing the autonomous value of earthly realities, respect for and attention to the secularity of the world. Ecclesiocentrism is thus surmounted in the sense of an ecclesiology that is missionary and political, dialogical and ministerial.

The Church as Communion

In describing the Church "inter tempora," "between times" — placed between its origin and its destiny as God's pilgrim people in time — Vatican II also rediscovered the basic theological value of the local church: this is the *Catholic Church*, i.e., the Church in the fullness of her mystery, made real in the concrete dimensions of space and time (cf. LG 26).

The motivation for this thesis lies in the Trinitarian origin of the Church, in its eucharistic nature and anthropological dimensions. The initiating action of the Trinity, made present by the Holy Spirit in the changing times, never becomes disembodied from human affairs; rather, it is decidedly present in them in order to bring them into salvation history. The Eucharist, in which Christ's passover is made present in the signs of the celebration as a memorial is celebrated only in the actual "here and now." The believers who make up the Church do not exist in the abstract, but only as members of a culture and heirs of a history in which the Church is built up (inculturation of the message). The fullness of the one, holy, catholic and apostolic Church is therefore realized, first and foremost, in the local church.

The unity of the local church has its highest expression and its wellspring in the Eucharist celebrated by the bishop with the body of priests and deacons and the active participation of all the faithful (LG 26). The variety of charisms and personal and communal ministries becomes part of and is coordinated in the local community, through the one Word, the one Bread, the one Spirit, by the bishop's ministry of unity and the exercise of all the other ministries. The bishop is the sign and minister (= servant) of the unity of the *Catholic Church*, made real in his local church (unity, diversity and communion).

The one Word, the one Bread, the one Spirit of the Risen Savior form the basis also for the unity among the different local churches. These local churches all represent the fullness of the mystery of the Church on the local level and, therefore, they are united among themselves. This communion is expressed by the collegial communion of their bishops, ministers and signs of their unity, around the Bishop of the Church who "presides in charity," viz., the Bishop of Rome, the minister of unity in the universal fellowship of the churches, each church truly and fully the Church in itself (locality, universality and communion).

2. The Church as People of God

2.1 People of God: Community, Charisms and Ministries

The visibilist conception of the Church, predominant in Catholic theology before the Second Vatican Council, led to emphasis on the hierarchical and pyramidal aspect of the reality of the Church. She was seen as a self-sufficient historical institution *(societas perfecta)*, with her own laws, her own rites and leaders, arranged in an orderly manner in a rigid system of dependence, with the multitude of the faithful *(societas inaequalis, hierarchica)* in subjection. Overemphasis was placed on hierarchical mediation: "In the hierarchy alone reside the right and authority needed to promote and direct all the members toward society's end. As for the multitude, they have no other right than that of letting themselves be led and submissively following their pastors."[1]

One widespread text, against which J. A. Moehler reacted firmly, stated: "God created the hierarchy and thus has more than sufficiently provided for the needs of the Church until the end of the world."[2]

Yves Congar characterized this conception as "hierarchological ecclesiology": "The Church was presented [...] as an organized society, consisting of the exercise of powers vested in the Pope, the bishops and priests. Ecclesiology consisted almost exclusively in a treatise on public law."[3]

The Council, receiving the fruits of the biblical, patristic and liturgical movement, restored the communal perspective of the early Church, characterized by the primacy of total ecclesiology: unity comes before distinction; the variety of ministries is rooted and nourished in the pneumatological and sacramental richness of the mystery of the Church. In the draft document *De Ecclesia,* the chapter on the People of God was inserted after that on the mystery of the Church and before the chapters on hierarchy and the laity. This insertion was "the first of those Copernican revolutions that characterized the drafting of the Constitution."[4]

It was motivated by these arguments, among others: "1. The Church is presented 'between times,' *(inter tempora)* on the journey toward the blessed goal, i.e., in her historical state [...]. 2. She is seen in her totality, according to what is common to all the faithful. And this is indispensable, so that it may expressly appear that the pastors and the faithful belong to a single people [...]. 3. We thus see more clearly both the task of the pastors, who offer the means of salvation, and the vocation of the faithful, who must personally collaborate in the spread and the sanctification of the entire Church [...]. In this way the idea of *service* stands out better. 4. In addition, we clearly see the *unity of the Church in a universal variety* of tasks, individual churches, traditions, cultures [...]. Far from destroying unity, these things enhance it."[5]

The Council's intention, as gleaned from these words, was to show "what is common to all the members of the People of God, before any distinction of office or particular state, considering the level of dignity of Christian existence."[6] That is to say, in the concept of the Church, primacy has been restored to the ontology of grace, which precedes and underlies all the particular divisions and subdivisions, thus highlighting Christian anthropology, i.e., "life according to the Spirit," who brings the newness of redeemed existence and makes it both an alternative and a proposal for every person. Within this rediscovery of total ecclesiology there is rediscovery also of the universal priesthood: "The baptized, by regeneration and the anointing of the Holy Spirit, are consecrated as a spiritual house and a holy priesthood, in order that through all those works which are those of the Christian people they may offer spiritual sacrifices and proclaim the power of him who has called them out of darkness into his marvelous light (cf. 1 Pet 2:4-10)" (LG 10).

The baptized person — no matter the charism received or the ministry exercised — is before all else the *homo christianus:* the person who through baptism has been incorporated into Christ (Christian from Christ), anointed by the Holy Spirit (Christ from *chrio* = I anoint) and consequently made one of the People of God. This means that all the baptized are the Church, partakers of the riches and responsibilities which that baptismal consecration involves. They have all been called to "present themselves as a living sacrifice, holy and acceptable to God (cf. Rom 12:1). Everywhere on earth they must bear witness to Christ and give an answer to those who seek an account of that hope of eternal life which is in them (cf. 1 Pet 3:15)" (LG 10).

In that perspective, the Council has rediscovered the charismatic dimension of the entire People of God, i.e., the richness and variety of gifts that the Holy Spirit pours into each baptized person for the benefit of all the members (LG 4 and 7), so that all may have a share — though according to different forms and services — in the prophecy, priesthood and kingship of the Lord Jesus.

While rediscovery of the primacy of total ecclesiology has been an authentic "ecclesiological shift," we must realize that Vatican II has not brought it to extreme consequences in noting the charismatic and ministerial variety among the People of God. The triple concept before the Council of "clerics-religious-laity" has of course become obsolete, thanks to the appropriate distinction between structures *of* the

Church (hierarchy-laity) and structures *in* the Church (religious life).[7]

Therefore, in *Lumen Gentium* the chapter on holiness was placed after the chapters on the hierarchy and the laity, to point up the common vocation to holiness of all the baptized; and before the chapter on religious, in order to characterize the religious state as a form of life open to all the faithful to achieve that vocation to holiness more freely. The Council, however, did not delve into the dynamism of life in the Church beyond the double pair of relationships: "hierarchy-laity" and "religious-nonreligious." At any rate, this double duality seems to be inadequate, in terms of the rich fabric of the anthropology of grace, which the Council wanted to highlight as the bedrock of any further specification. The development of postconciliar reflection shows that fidelity to the "shift" made by the Council requires here going beyond the Council itself. For what reasons? In what direction?

The dual term "hierarchy-laity" refers to the difference in essence and not only in degree between the common priesthood and the ministerial priesthood, also to the interrelation between them: "Though they differ from one another in essence and not only in degree, the common priesthood of the faithful and the ministerial or hierarchical priesthood, are nonetheless related: each of them in its own special way, is a participation in the one priesthood of Christ" (LG 10).

The formula *essentia et non gradu tantum,* (by

essence and not only by degree) used in the conciliar text, should be interpreted according to its historical genesis: it reverts to an allocution of Pius XII in 1954.[8] In that text the formula is used to refute any idea of delegation or equality in the relationship between community and sacred ministers. The reference to the historical genesis explains how the formula can say too much and say too little. It says too much if we read it according to the ordinary current usage of the word *essence.* In that sense it connotes almost an abyss between the two priesthoods. It says too little if we read it according to the Scholastic language in which it was originally formulated. In that sense, essence denotes every mode of existence. The formula here says nothing more than that each of the two priesthoods has its own specific nature, without thereby defining that specific nature.

The first interpretation, which puts the difference at extremes, is unacceptable in the light of Vatican II. The Council sees one priesthood as being interrelated with the other. The second interpretation needs to be clarified by shedding light on the specific nature of the ministerial priesthood in terms of the fullest ministry of the Church. This specific nature cannot be characterized by a greater or lesser intensity of participation in the one priesthood of Christ (for then the difference would be one of degree!) On the basis of this participation common to all, the foundation of unity preceding any distinction, the different forms of ministry are to be singled out. These represent in a different way the one Shepherd, Priest and Prophet.

Thus, Christ the Head, minister of the unity of his ecclesial body, is represented by the ordained ministry, established so that the faithful may be "united together in one body in which 'all the members do not have the same function' (Rom 12:4)" *(Presbyterorum Ordinis,* 2).

"To accomplish its mission, the Church needs persons who will publicly and consistently take responsibility to manifest the Church's basic dependence on Jesus Christ. In this way they will supply, within a multiplicity of gifts, a focal point of her unity. The ministry of those persons, who from very early times have been ordained, is constitutive of the Church's life and witness."[9]

This ministry, however, does not exhaust the Church's ministries. It does not represent the *whole Christ.* The ordained minister, precisely because he acts *"in persona Christi capitis,"* in the name of *Christ the Head* (PO 2), i.e., because he is a minister of unity, calls attention to the other members of the body, to the variety of the gifts and services raised up by the Holy Spirit. A ministry of synthesis, it must not become a synthesis of ministries (the concept of "clericalizing"), but a service of discernment and coordination of charisms and ministries in view of fellowship and growth, a service exercised through the triple prophetic, priestly and pastoral function by the local bishop for the entire local church, and by the priest and deacons in the fields of action entrusted to them by the bishop. The fruit of a gift from the Holy Spirit, which is powerfully realized in the sacramental act of ordination, the ordained ministry is at the service of the Spirit. It should be welcomed again and again, to "test everything; hold fast what is good" (1 Thes 5:21).

Because of this service it renders to the unity and development of the ecclesial body, the ordained ministry is established from the very origins of the Christian Church, though in a variety of forms, to last until Christ returns, and to be in the Church and for the Church, but never outside the Church or separate from it. As for the other ministries in the Church, each of them will enrich the ministry of unity with its own charism. When this charism, even if not united to a sacramental consecration, is directed toward a definite service that is constantly and vitally needed for the community, is carried out with true responsibility, and is recognized by the Church through some act of institution, we speak of an "instituted" ministry. However, when the charism is joined to a significant service for the community, but one which is not constant, i.e., it may pass away with changing needs or situations, we speak of a "de facto" ministry.

In any case, the ministry appears to be a charism in a state of service, received by the community. And the charismatic wealth of the Church Body, by reason of the action of the Spirit, is such that we may say that the entire Church is ministerial and that the personal or even communal forms (movements, associations, and so forth) of ministry by themselves never exhaust the possibilities of the gifts the faithful receive in baptism. The entire ministerial Church is nothing but the Church completely filled with the action of the Holy Spirit and completely engaged in service. The inadequate dual term "hierarchy-laity" is thus supplanted by another dual term, which indicates above all the total unity and, within that unity, the well-ordered diversity of services: the dual term "community-ministries."[10]

If the term "hierarchy-laity" distinguishes too much, because it overshadows the ontology of grace common to all, and distinguishes too little, because it reduces the Church's array of ministries to the single form of ordained ministry, considering the others negatively (lay persons = non-clerics), in the dual term "community-ministries" the baptismal community is like an encompassing reality. Within that reality the ministries are arrayed as services in view of what the entire Church must be and do. In this way we see more clearly that the relationship between ministries, whether ordained or not, is not a relationship of one ministry superior to the others, but of one ministry that complements another in diversity, of service that is reciprocal with invariable differences. The Church, the icon of the Trinity, is one in the mystery of the Water, the Bread, the Word and the Spirit, and is different in the rich bounty of its gifts and services.

The other dual term which Vatican II uses in the presentation on the People of God—this time in reference to the structures *in* the Church—is "religious-nonreligious": both categories may include lay persons and ordained ministers. That is to say, the

distinction is not based on a different form of relationship to Christ (Head or Body), but on a different state
of life, with a view to the common goal of holiness.
The foundation of religious life remains — as for
every Christian — baptismal consecration. Here, too,
unity precedes distinction, and the latter has a func-
tional value in terms of the *following of Christ,*
according to the vocation given to each person by the
Holy Spirit. This dual term does not bring out the
priority of fundamental unity. The anthropology of
grace is overshadowed by emphasis on the diversity
of states of life, a diversity very relative as compared
with the unity of baptismal consecration and of our
vocation to holiness.

Here too, therefore, we have to acquire a different
understanding of the relationships within the Church,
wherein the common Christian condition, the Holy
Spirit's free and varied activity in it, the charismatic
nature of every state of life and its purposeful place in
the Church are made more evident. The dual term
"community-charisms and ministries" seems to meet
these requirements. In the encompassing reality of
the new People of God, this term embodies the variety
of gifts, given freely by the Holy Spirit for the benefit
of all and taking on forms of ministry in personal and
community life, which correspond to the different
states (e.g., married or celibate; religious or nonre-
ligious).

The pair of dual terms with which the Council
presents the different relationships within the People
of God ("hierarchy-laity": Chapters III and IV of

Lumen Gentium; "religious-nonreligious": Chapter VI) therefore seems inadequate. The rediscovery of the ministerial nature of the whole Church and of the even greater charismatic richness that underlies it, joined to the recovery of the total ecclesiology, contends against so limited an expression in relation to ministry or states of life. We have to carry through to its ultimate consequences the primacy that the Council accorded to the ontology of grace in respect to any further specification within it. In this light, use of the dual term "community-charisms and ministries" cannot be reduced to a simple shift of accent or play on words. It reflects, rather, a radical turnabout to be made in the Church's conception and practice. It is a matter of going from a pyramidal and hierarchological ecclesiology, wherein there is a visible hierarchical mediation between Christ and the baptized, to an ecclesiology of communion, wherein the pneumatological dimension is given first place. Here, the Holy Spirit is seen as acting upon the entire community to make of it the Body of Christ, raising up in that community a host of charisms. These charisms then take form in a variety of ministries at the service of the growth of the community.

The entire Church is thus looked upon as something dynamic: she has not been established once and for all and made self-sufficient until the end of time through the hierarchical institution that provides for everything; rather, she is being continually raised up and renewed by the fidelity of the Holy Spirit, who continues in history "by no weak analogy" (LG 8) the mystery of the Incarnation.

Putting into a broader context the distinction of the People of God into two classes, typical of the Middle Ages, does not of course mean acceptance of an undifferentiated confusion. No longer thinking of the Church in the sole relationship of hierarchy-laity does not imply a watering down of her theological representation and life. On the contrary, we want to enrich them, extending to all the baptized in an explicit way the responsibility of being "church" and of expressing in their lives a dimension of service to which the Church is called, in well-ordered and fruitful communion with all the other possible expressions.

By rising above the category of "lay state," we are freed from the awkward search for a positive specific quality to be conveyed by the term "lay person," whereas we promote the necessary and creative definition of different forms of ministry. In the Church there are, and must be to an ever greater degree, many ministries. These ministries will express the gift and commitment proper to each baptized person. But the lay state — as a category that is the opposite of the clergy or the religious life — exists only as a negative abstraction, which diminishes the dynamism of life in the Church. Lay people must therefore become aware of their consecration and mission by virtue of baptism and the work of the Holy Spirit. In addition, ordained ministers must be well aware that they are not everything in the Church. Thus both can make up a well-ordered communion, in which each person is called to bring his or her own original and irreplaceable contribution. On a practical level, this is the way opened by the rediscovery of total ecclesiology: the way of a new maturity of baptized persons. It is based on each person's awareness of his or her own Christian dignity and the responsibility of all the faithful to discern their particular charisms so as to put them at the service of the entire People of God.

2.2   People of God and Laicity of the Whole Church

The surmounting of the division of the People of God into two classes, together with recovery of a total ecclesiology, is joined to the positive conception of "laicity" as a dimension of the entire Church present in history. Laicity is an "affirmation of the autonomy and permanence of the secular world compared with the religious domain. I am referring to life in the world."[11]

Laicity in that sense is the same as "secularity," in recognition of the value proper to the *saeculum,* to reality as a whole, the earthly relations and choices that characterize the daily existence of everyone. In the history of ecclesiology, laicity has been viewed in different ways, which reflect the different concepts of the Church herself.

One initial perspective was rejection of laicity: this is the attitude of ecclesiocentrism. According to this perspective the Church is a "perfect society." She is self-sufficient for her needs and, in relation to the world, her attitude must be one of teaching and judging. Earthly values are not recognized for what they are in themselves, but measured and criticized in relation to the "eternal truths," entrusted through Revelation to the deposit of which the Church is the keeper and custodian. *Domini et magistra,* the Church draws from these truths judgments on every possible question that history puts to her, according to a monolithic logic that presumes to have the answers to everything. It has been rightly noted that this attitude has isolated the Church from the modern world. It has facilitated the process of secularization, set in motion by the "liberating rationality" of the Enlightenment: "The reality of a Godless world, which we are now facing, is in part only a reaction to a worldless God."[12]

This representation of its external relationships *(ad extra)* was reflected also in the Church's way of looking at and doing things *ad intra* (within herself). The rejection of the autonomy of the mundane was joined to a heavy accentuation of the sacred. In relationships within the Church, this devolved into the absolutizing of hierarchical mediation, i.e., of that "sacred power" which was considered the guardian and dispenser of the sacred. Thus, in contrast to the teaching Church, active in her magisterium and in her sacramental and pastoral work, was the *learning* Church, consisting of the simple faithful, whose main task was to listen, obey and let themselves be led. A Church closed to laicity in her relationship to the world becomes a Church that is clerical within herself, in which lay people are only described as "nonclerical."

In reaction to that attitude, a regeneration of laicity within ecclesiology has been at work. In terms of the Church/world relationship this has meant the development of that theology of earthly realities which emerged in the Schema 13 of Vatican II. We know how the change in the title of that document ("De Ecclesia *et* mundo hujus temporis" became "De Ecclesia *in* mundo hujus temporis"): "On the Church *and* the Modern World" became "On the Church *in* the Modern World" spelled a significant change in mentality. Church and world were no longer seen as two separate poles more or less in competition with each other. Clearly, it affirmed the need for a Church present amid earthly realities like a yeast and enzyme, recognizing the proper and positive value of these realities. From a monolithic attitude, according to which the world could only be the recipient of the proclamation and of the judgment of the Gospel, a movement was under way toward dialogue, in which the Church appears as the one that teaches, but also as one that listens and learns.

The theological foundation of this different relationship lay in the Christic dimension of all creation ("All things were created through him and for him," Col 1:16) and in the cosmic dimension of the Incarnation (if "that which has not been taken on has not been saved, either," everything has been taken on so that everything may be saved). The world, recognized as the place of the Gospel, became a partner in the dialogue of salvation: besides reading history "in the light of" the Gospel, an effort was made to also read the Gospel in history.

This different conception of the relationship between Church and laicity was reflected also in the image of the Church *ad intra*. In recovering the primacy of total ecclesiology, we recognized the dignity and self-determination proper to every baptized person and, hence, the specific responsibility of lay people. Vatican II spelled out for them the lay state in a special way, in the wake of theological efforts to define its characteristic feature: "What specifically characterizes lay people is their secular nature. It is true that those in Holy Orders can at times be engaged in secular activities, and even have a secular profession. But they are, by reason of their particular vocation, especially and professedly ordained to the sacred ministry. Similarly, by their state in life, religious give splendid and striking testimony that the world cannot be transformed and offered to God without the spirit of the Beatitudes. But the laity, by their very vocation, seek the kingdom of God by engaging in temporal affairs and by ordering them according to the plan of God" (LG 31).

Laicity is therefore seen to be within the Church as a dimension that characterizes the entire People of God, except for ordained ministers and religious. The historical origins of this connection between secularity and lay people are rooted in the late Constantinian period. At that time, standing in contrast to the clerics and monks who were given to spiritual things and increasingly close to each other, were the lay people, involved in the world.[13]

Also rooted in this contrast is the lay spirit, which would be fully affirmed in the modern age as an attitude of independence from the religious sphere, an attitude often marked by a tone of controversy or rejection toward that religious sphere. In the early centuries of the Christian experience, however, it was different: the Church as a whole was viewed as an alternative to the world. The distinction was perceived not so much *ad intra* between "spiritual souls" and Christians given to temporal things, as *ad extra* between a Christian newness common to all the baptized, and a society to be evangelized.

The rediscovery of this newness, together with recovery of the primacy of an integral ecclesiology, implies the need to surmount not only the division of the Church into two classes but also the specific connection of "lay people-secularity." If all the baptized receive the Holy Spirit to give him to the world, all have the responsibility in the temporal order to announce the Gospel and vitalize history. We cannot characterize the laity only by their relationship to laicity. By surmounting the double duality of "hierarchy-laity" and "religious-nonreligious" with the dual term "community-charisms and ministries," we not only restore primacy to the ontology of grace but see rooted in it a mission to the world and, hence, the task of evangelical vitalization of what is secular.

The relationship with temporal realities is proper

to all the baptized, though in a variety of forms, joined more to personal charisms than to static contrasts between laity, hierarchy and religious state. Not to be aware that all the conditions of life, even within the Church, have an earthly and political-social dimension actually implies an attitude filled with earthly and political-social overtones, as history demonstrates. No one is neutral toward the historical circumstances in which he or she is living, and an alleged neutrality can easily become a voluntary or involuntary mask for ideologies and special interests. We must therefore — developing the premises of Vatican II — arrive at a different understanding of laicity in ecclesiology. By virtue of that understanding laicity is neither rejected as in the monolithic attitude nor considered as a single component of Church reality. It is the entire community that has to confront the secular world, being marked by that world in its being and in its action. The entire People of God must be characterized by a positive relationship with the secular dimension.

What is implied in this understanding of laicity as a dimension proper to the entire Church community? Certainly, a noncritical and undifferentiated understanding of laicity is easily transformed into reducing the original force of the Gospel to the dimensions of this world. A counter-reaction to ecclesiocentrism can be ecclesiopragmatism, in which the secular aspect of the Church is so accentuated as to undermine the original and irreducible identity of her Trinitarian origin and goal. If the People of God is delivered from the monolithic temptation and ends up being relegated to historical irrelevance, the sense of the Christian alternative is likely to become warped and reduced to an exclusively earthly horizon. We need to have an understanding of laicity as a dimension proper to the whole Church, without secularistic reductions and jumbled confusion whereby the ecclesial identity and specific nature of the different charisms and ministries are undermined in the name of a supposedly more telling historical presence.

A critical understanding of laicity within total ecclesiology hinges on three issues: first, that of intra-ecclesial relations (laicity within the Church); then, on the issue of the common responsibility of the baptized toward what is secular and of the mediation needed between salvation and history (laicity of the Church); lastly, on the question of the Church's recognition of the proper and independent value of earthly realities (the laicity of the world respected and accepted by the Church).

First of all, *laicity in the Church* means respect for the value of what is most deeply, most truly human: the baptized are persons whose dignity and responsibility must be recognized and promoted. Human rights — the highest expression of laicity in its authentic sense — are an absolute and inalienable value, also in terms of relations within the Church; there is no authority — not even a sacred one — who is authorized to disregard them. Acceptance of laicity in the Church makes us look askance at the too ready use of power that one person can exercise over another in the name of the sacred. The self-determination and creativity of individuals must not be repressed in the name of an absolute and unmotivated obedience; the right of freedom of inquiry, of expression, and of different historical-political choices must not be sacrificed in the name of an unqualified Church discipline.

The proper climate of laicity in the Church is that of tolerance and dialogue. It is based theologically on an ecclesiology of the priestly People of God which, in recognizing the proper and original work of the one Spirit in each baptized person, sees unity as being enriched and not debased by diversity. In this sense, laicity in the Church comes to mean freedom of the Christian, primacy of conscience and interior motivation as regards formal observance, the responsibility of each person for the growth of the community toward the fullness of divine truth (cf. *Dei Verbum* 8).

We must therefore rise above the contrast between teaching Church and learning Church, in the sense of the active component and the passive component of the People of God. All believers by virtue of their baptismal dignity and according to the charism received and the ministry exercised, form both a Church that teaches and a Church that learns, a Church that receives and a Church that gives the Holy Spirit. In this light, the traditional doctrine of the *sense of the faithful (sensus)* and *universal agreement* of the faithful *(consensus fidelium)* is like a true opening to an understanding of laicity in the life of the Church (cf. LG 12).

In the second place, *laicity of the Church* means

the responsibility of all the baptized (and not only of lay people) toward the temporal order. In this sense, laicity springs from the ordination to service and mission inherent in the anthropology of grace. All baptized persons are called to become present in the historical situation in which they live, exercising the critical-prophetic role that the encounter between the Word of God and the present enkindles in them. This entails putting aside the idea of apostolate of the laity as "cooperation with the hierarchical apostolate" of the Church. Actually, all Christians, each one according to his or her individual charism, must cooperate with others in the evangelization of the community and of history. All have a part to play, both within the life of the Church and in contact with the world, by committing themselves to put their gifts into service where the Holy Spirit calls each one of them, in a relationship of well-ordered and dynamic fellowship amid the various ministries and charisms.

In this perspective there is no longer a separation between the sacred and the profane: if the Spirit blows where he wills, it is not possible to limit his action with extrinsic categories. If the lordship of God embraces the whole person and life itself, every worldly situation is capable of being lived in relation to the promise of the faith and, therefore, assessed and guided by the "eschatological reserve" proper to the Christian. There are no separate spheres — the sacred and the profane, God and Caesar — for which each person has recourse to specialists (sacred ministers and lay people). There is the one sphere of existence, with a complexity of definite relations that make up history. In these relations a Christian must place himself, whatever his charism or ministry may be, in terms of the autonomy of earthly realities ("Render therefore to Caesar the things that are Caesar's") and in a permanent openness to the disquieting horizon of the Kingdom ("and to God the things that are God's").

The twofold transcending — of the separation between agents (lay people — ordained ministers — religious) and the spheres (the sacred and the profane) of relationship between the Church and the temporal — therefore defines the laicity of the Church as a shared responsibility of all the baptized in the process of mediation between salvation and history, as a presence of Christians in human affairs, capable of joining fidelity to the present world with fidelity to the world to come, without merging one with the other.

The concept of the Church, which comes across through these indications, is that of a missionary and "political" ecclesiology. In that ecclesiology, the decisive role of the Christian community's relationship *ad extra* (as in the Church of the martyrs!) is re-established. In that ecclesiology, all the baptized, considered even in the different structures proper to them, are seen as projected outside of themselves, toward the world to which they have been sent, marked by laicity in their being and in their actions.

Lastly, a critical understanding of laicity in ecclesiology implies recognition by the Church of the proper and autonomous value of earthly realities, respect for and attention to the *secularity of the world*.

Ecclesiocentrism must be transcended here through an ecclesiology of dialogue and ministry: a Church that is poor and serving, in dialogue and in the service of all the people, recognizes that it is not the exclusive repository of truth. Rather, it opens up to the dignity and freedom of every human person, of every historical situation, to take in their genuine values while proposing the word of the Gospel.

This calls for an objective, though critically watchful, attitude toward different cultures. While it will always be necessary to reject any identification between message and culture so as not to render Christian "scandal" meaningless, it will also be necessary to single out what is proper and genuine in each cultural world so as to put it in real and mutually fruitful contact with the Gospel. It is not possible to proceed by deduction from Revelation to a variety of historical situations, seeking in the message an already prepared answer to the questions and urgent needs of the present. It is always necessary to experience the toil of mediation, wherein the terms to be related—culture and the Gospel, salvation and history—are taken seriously in their reciprocal autonomy and their reciprocal points of conflict. Only at this price will there be inculturation of the message, without which the proclaiming of God's kingdom sounds empty or meaningless; only at this price will there be a catholicity of the People of God, understood as its vocation to fullness, which is found in Christ.

Without careful and critical acceptance of the

world's laicity, without open and calm dialogue with the people we meet in the world, the Word remains suffocated. It is in this acceptance and this dialogue, however, that the Word unleashes its critical and liberating force upon all human situations. The ecclesiology of dialogue and service is not a loss of the Church's identity, but a rediscovery of that identity on the highest level, precisely, the Gospel requirement of "losing" one's own life to "save" it (cf. Mt 10:39). Acceptance of the world's laicity thus becomes a dimension that the People of God cannot put aside, for this People is called to be a presence of salvation among others, in the concreteness of the space and time of history.

3. The Church as Communion

3.1 The Ecclesiology of Communion

The rediscovery of the Trinitarian foundation of the Church, by virtue of which the Trinity is the origin, form and goal of the reality of the Church, brings us to a consideration – in presenting God's pilgrim people *inter tempora,* between the time of the Church's origin and the time of the heavenly homeland – of the idea of "communion," i.e., unity in catholic variety. To bring to fulfillment his plan of unity amid a variety of people and nations, the Father has sent his Son and the Holy Spirit, the Lord and Lifegiver. "He it is who brings together the whole Church and each and every one of those who believe, and who is the wellspring of their unity in the teaching of the apostles and in fellowship, in the breaking of bread and in prayers (cf. Ac 2:42)" (LG 13).

This idea of fellowship made real by the Holy

Spirit in the faithful through the Word and the Bread is contained in a very old expression of the Faith, present in the creedal formulas after the mention of the Holy Spirit and the Holy Catholic Church: "sanctorum communio." Analyzing the structure of the Creed, which is a narration of the Trinitarian history of God for us, first, of the Father ("I believe in God, the Father Almighty..."), then — more palpable and full because built on the Gospel account — of the Son ("and in one Lord, Jesus Christ...") and, lastly, of the Holy Spirit ("I believe in the Holy Spirit..."), we note that the Church is mentioned directly in the narration on the work of the Comforter. This makes evident the levels of depth of the expression "communio sanctorum."

The narration makes reference above all to the Holy Spirit, the Lord and Lifegiver of Church communion ("communio Sancti": communion of the Holy One), then, to the holy realities, through which the Spirit communicates himself, viz., the Word, the Water and the Bread ("communio sanctorum": "communion of 'holy things,' of the sacraments," in the sense of the neuter genitive plural = "communio sacramentorum"); and lastly, to the faithful, who have been touched by the Paraclete and imbued with his love, and by him made one in the variety of gifts offered to each person ("communio sanctorum": communion of saints in the sense of the personal genitive plural = "communio sanctorum fidelium"; "communion of holy faithful people").[1] These three levels of meaning in the expression "sanctorum communio" thus express the three levels of attainment of fellow-ship, which is the Church.

The Church is above all a "communio Sancti," fellowship in the Spirit of Christ: coming from the Trinity, it is not a human work, but the fruit of God's initiating action, the work of the Spirit of God. For this fundamental reason, ecclesial communion is a "mystery," i.e., it is not reducible to sociological categories or to strictly historical or political evalu-ations. It cannot be relegated to the realm of a mere earthly horizon, and it offers itself as the presence in history of what is beyond history, of the divine which, entering into the flesh of the world, both kills it and restores it to life, judges it in its frail state, and redeems it in eternity. The communion (koinonia) which is the Church at once holy and sinful, bears within itself the signs of this amazing encounter between the world of the Spirit and the world of humankind. Hence, totally immersed in history and in the contradictions of human affairs, the Church is called to bring to them the tidings and gift of God's new world, revealed in Jesus Christ.

The task of the Church is therefore that of making present in every age and in every situation the coming together of the Spirit and the flesh, of God and the human family, as embodied in the Word Incarnate. Even as it receives the Spirit through Christ from the Father, ecclesial fellowship is called to give him to others. Its mission is summed up in the mandate to bring the entire universe to the Father through Christ in the one Holy Spirit. The Church as fellowship is the sign and instrument, or rather the sacrament, through which the Holy Spirit brings about the unity of people with God and among themselves.

The Church is, therefore, a fellowship in holy realities ("communio sanctorum sacramentorum"), which makes it a sacrament of Christ, as Christ is the sacrament of God. This total and sacramental quality of ecclesial fellowship is expressed in two very special ways: the Word of God, which, by judging and enlightening us, calls us to salvation; and the Sacrament, the greatest form of embodiment of the Word, the re-presentation of Christ's paschal mystery in the lives of the faithful. Both Word and Sacrament are present in the highest degree and converge at the Lord's Supper. As the memorial of Christ's passover, i.e., the commemoration of it in a diversity of times and places, the Eucharist reconciles people with God and with each other. "The eucharistic communion with Christ present, which nourishes the life of the Church, is at the same time a communion in the Body of Christ which is the Church. The sharing of the one bread and of the one chalice, in a given place, manifests and completes the unity of the participants with Christ and all the communicants, in every time and place."[2]

The Eucharist is the "sacramentum unitatis," the one bread from which is born the one Body of Christ, which is the Church, in the power of the Holy Spirit. Word and bread are in the Eucharist the sacrament from which ecclesial communion is born: the Eucharist makes the Church, fellowship in the holy realities given in the celebration of the eucharistic memorial. While the Eucharist makes the Church, it is also true that the Church makes the Eucharist: the Word is not proclaimed if there is no one to preach it (cf. Rom 10:14-15); the memorial is not celebrated if there is no one who celebrates it in obedience to the Lord's command. Both Word and sacrament require the ministries of the Church, the service of preaching, the service of celebrating the sacrifice, and the service of bringing the dispersed human family together into the unity of God's holy people: "The Church is a gathering of holy people, in which the Gospel is purely taught and the sacraments are rightly administered."[3]

Ecclesial fellowship is totally ministerial, totally called – in a variety of ministries – to a triple task that is prophetic, priestly and royal. Every baptized person is formed by the Holy Spirit in the likeness of Christ the Prophet, Priest and Shepherd and, therefore, is committed, in fellowship with others in the ministry of unity, which is the ordained ministry, to herald in this life the Word of God, to celebrate the memorial of the Last Supper, and to bring about in history the justice of God's Kingdom to come.

This commitment, founded on the gifts that the Holy Spirit lavishes on each person, is exercised in the different ministerial, personal or communal forms. The ministry is nothing other than a charism linked to a task, transformed into a service to the community, which the community recognizes and receives. The entire ministerial Church is nothing other than the entire charismatic fellowship of the baptized in its condition of service.

Lastly, the Church is the communion of "saints" ("communio sanctorum fidelium"). Christian life, brought forth in the womb of our Holy Mother the Church through the Word of God and the sacraments, is life according to the Spirit: "For all who are led by the Spirit of God are children of God" (Rom 8:14). A Christian is the Holy Spirit's anointed. In baptism and in the sacramental economy the Christian is conformed to Christ, and through him and in him is filled with the Holy Spirit. The Church is the communion of "saints" precisely in the sense that the baptized have a share in the one Holy Spirit and are enriched by the variety of the Spirit's gifts. These gifts are given unceasingly by the Spirit, who distributes them to each person as he wills. They are called "charisms," i.e., free gifts, the fruit of the freedom and creativity of the Consoler, bestowed by him with superabundant richness and intended for the growth of Christ's Body, the Church: "To each is given the manifestation of the Spirit for the common good" (1 Cor 12:7).

Every Christian is a "charismatic" if he recognizes and accepts God's gift: the Spirit's imagination is inexhaustible; the Spirit's work is unremitting. No baptized person has a right to time off, because each person is individually endowed with charisms to be lived out in service and in fellowship. No one has a right to separation, because charisms come from the one Spirit and are intended to build up the one Body of the Lord, which is the Church (cf. 1 Cor 12:4-7). No one has a right to stand still or to pine for the past, for the Spirit is always alive and active. The Spirit is the newness of God and the Lord of future time.

As a result we have the style of a Church, the communion of "saints": it must be open to the Spirit and to the Spirit's surprises. Always in quest of victory over the tragic resistance of personal and social sin, "always in need of renewal and purification," it must be docile in discerning the Spirit, especially in those who have received the charism of discernment and coordination of charisms: the ordained ministers.

This openness to new things from God must always be accompanied by a deep sense of responsibility. If all have received the Spirit, all must communicate the Spirit, committing themselves in shared responsibility with others for the Church's growth in communion and in service. While the Church as communion is not a field of dead people but of people alive in the Spirit, neither is it a place for individual adventures: fidelity to the Spirit calls for courageous and patient growth in fellowship with everyone. The courage of the prophets is also and always the humble love of the "saints"!

3.2   The "Priority" of the Local Church in the Ecclesiology of Communion

The Church as communion comes from the Trinity, reflects in herself a Trinitarian communion that is one in diversity, and advances toward the Trinity, in the final gathering of all things in Christ, so that he may deliver them to the Father in the communion of Glory. Ecclesial communion is the place of encounter of the Trinitarian history of God and human history in which one passes continually into the other to transform it and give it life and in which the affairs of this world are brought to their fulfillment in God.

This condition of being a place of covenant, a sign of the Trinity in man's time here on earth, requires that the Church be solidly situated in the unfolding affairs of humankind. The initiating action and fidelity of the triune God are not directed to an abstract, nonexistent history, but to a definite, concrete history, to "histories" that develop in a definite time and space. It is in those histories that the work of the Spirit enters, pouring forth from the Father through the Son and always about to return through the Son to the Father. It is the Spirit who makes the Holy Trinity present here and now, and it is in the Spirit that every fragment of space and time has access to the Trinitarian mystery of the Church's origin.

The Spirit guarantees the seriousness and concern with which the God of Christians looks upon human history and makes that history his own. The Spirit is the historical dimension of the mystery: he gives this to the Church. We thus understand how, if "Christomonism" laid stress on the universal structured unity of believers, the Trinitarian and pneumatological rediscovery ushered in by Vatican II has led us to devote full attention to the local church, the community raised up in the *here and now* by God's initiative operating in the Spirit. Pneumatological renewal and recovery of the paramount value of the local church thus appear inseparable.

The Spirit's action, however, fostering fellowship in the space and time of a definite historical situation, does not take place invisibly, outside or against the logic of the Incarnation. If Christ is not to be separated from the Spirit ("Christomonism"), neither should the Spirit be separated from Christ (as in a certain Pentecostal type of congregationalism). The Spirit event never takes place apart from the Christ event; rather, it re-presents and updates it in the variety of human affairs. The special places where the Spirit rushes in are the ones that Christ has indicated and entrusted to his followers, i.e., the Word and the living signs of the new covenant. The one that embodies them all and that, compared with the others, stands out as the source and summit of the Church's life (cf. *Sacrosanctum Concilium* 10) is the celebration of the Eucharist. In the holy memorial of the Lord's Supper, Christ, dead and risen, is made present through the Word and the Spirit to reconcile people with the Father and with each other.

In the Eucharist, the opposite temptations – "Christomonist" and "Pentecostal-Congregationalist" – are engaged and surmounted. The Eucharist is an event of the Spirit and also an institution of Christ, faithfully transmitted by the Church; it is something charismatic and new as well as a continuity of the "traditio ecclesiae" (tradition of the Church) ministerially structured; it is the "already" imparted by the Lord and also a pledge of the "not yet" of his promise. In this double sense (pneumatological and Christological) the following statement can be included: the Eucharist makes the Church and the Church makes the Eucharist.

The Eucharist makes the Church in that it is the place where the Spirit rushes in: it re-presents Christ's Last Supper and thus gathers together his followers by virtue of the reconciliation it brings about. The Church makes the Eucharist in that it is the celebrating community which, in obedience to the Lord's command, comes together in its ministerial formation to celebrate the memorial of the new covenant. Therefore, Christian faith has looked upon the Eucharist as the sacrament of unity and used the same term to designate the Eucharist and the Church: "Corpus Christi," the Body of the Lord.

Now, by its nature the Eucharist is joined to a particular celebrating community, to a definite place and time: the Church that is born and expresses itself in the Eucharist is therefore, by priority, the *local* church. Even as in the celebration of the passover banquet the fullness of Christ's mystery is offered to us, so in the local eucharistic community, with the bishop presiding according to the oldest Christian tradition, the fullness of the ecclesial mystery is present, i.e., the "Catholic Church" is made real *hic et nunc* (here and now). This is energetically expressed in a particular conciliar text that really sums up eucharistic ecclesiology. One finds it, almost unexpectedly, in the context of Chapter III of *Lumen Gentium*: "A bishop, marked with the fullness of the sacrament of Orders, is 'the steward of the grace of the supreme priesthood,' especially in the Eucharist, which he offers or causes to be offered, and by which the Church continually lives and grows. This Church of Christ is truly present [*vere adest*] in all legitimate local congregations of the faithful which, united with their pastors, are themselves called churches in the New Testament. For in their locality these are the new People called by God, in the Holy Spirit and in much fullness (cf. 1 Thes 1:5). In them the faithful are gathered together by the preaching of the Gospel of Christ, and the mystery of the Lord's Supper is celebrated, 'that by the food and blood of the Lord's body the whole brotherhood may be joined together.' In any community of the altar, under the sacred ministry of the bishop, there is exhibited a symbol of that charity and 'unity of the Mystical Body, without which there can be no salvation.' In these communities, though frequently small and poor, or living far from any other, Christ is present, and in virtue of his presence, there is brought together the one, holy, catholic and apostolic Church" (LG 26).[4]

The local eucharistic community, gathered under the presiding bishop, the sign and minister of the unity of the local church, is one through the one Spirit and the one Body of Christ, who build it up. It is holy by virtue of the same Spirit, who sanctifies it. It is catholic because it represents in fullness (*kath'olou*) the mystery of the Lord, who is present in history, bringing about reconciliation with the Father. It is apostolic because it is set in the continuity of the apostolic tradition of obedience to the command of Jesus: "Do this in remembrance of me," and it is structured ministerially so as to fulfill the apostolic mission. In terms of eucharistic ecclesiology, therefore, there are no parts or portions of the Church: the one ecclesial Body of Christ is present in full in the individual local eucharistic communities, which are *the* Church, embodied in a definite time and definite place.

The priority of the local church in the ecclesiology of communion is thus grounded in the Trinitarian and pneumatological origin of the Church and its eucharistic nature; however, there is an anthropological consideration to be taken into account in our assessment of the local church. People never exist *in vitro*. They exist only in flesh and blood, situated in actual relationships of interdependence, rooted in a history and in a culture.

To these people the Word of salvation is preached, and this must be done in such a way that it can be understood and accepted. Precisely because it is the "word of God for us men and for our salvation," the message should be "culturally adapted," i.e., rendered in the forms and terms of the historical and cultural tradition in which it is preached, but without being reduced to those categories and hence emptied of its dynamic originality. Rather, it must function as a liberating criticism of cultures. The Church comes forth from the preaching of the "culturally adapted"

Word, particularly in the greatest form of embodiment of that Word, which is the Eucharist celebrated in the concrete dimensions of space and time. Hence, it must itself be "culturally adapted" in its makeup, i.e., situated precisely and originally in the history of its people, the "local" church. For it speaks the language of its nation, thinks in the categories of the people of that nation, experiences the tensions and contradictions they experience, and causes to resound in those tensions and contradictions the lifegiving power of the Gospel.

From the anthropological standpoint, too, the Church is seen first of all in its local aspect, the place of encounter between the reality of salvation given in Christ and a definite situation, with all the natural, social and cultural features that characterize it. Therefore, from the very beginning the Church has existed only *concretely* as the Church of God which is at Corinth, at Antioch, at Rome....

The priority of the local church in the ecclesiology of communion is rooted in the initiating action of the Trinity, in the Eucharist and in anthropology. As a result of that priority, we have to recognize the local church as being by full right the "ecclesial subject." This implies not only an indispensable autonomy, which is required to express and nourish its own ecclesial vitality, but the conviction that there is no authentic dimension to the life of the Church unless it is first a *local* dimension.

Here we note the force of the teaching on the sacramental nature of the episcopacy, affirmed by

Vatican II (LG 21), which joins to the very dignity of the bishop the dignity of the local church. Here we note the significance of an actual decentralization of the Church, of a real exercise of the principle of subsidiarity. According to that principle, what can be done on the local level (and it is truly much!) must not be done on another level. Here we note, too, the theological inconsistency of the idea of the Church as a "sectarian body," an historical superstructure that can undermine the rich and manifold variety of the local churches.

In short, there is no truly ecclesial act that was not originally the act of a local church. The negative side to this principle is that any structure or initiative whatsoever, directed toward fellowship and mission, is not authentically *ecclesial* unless it is rooted in and related to the local church or local churches. In other words, the alternative is not between local church and universal Church, but between local church and non-existence of the Church.

Just as there is a priority of the local church on the level of communion, there is a priority of the local church on the level of mission, by virtue of the bond between fellowship and mission, which is the icon of the relationship between Trinitarian communion and the divine missions (cf. Chapter I of the decree *Ad Gentes*). The entire local church is sent to preach the whole Gospel to the whole person, to every person. This statement shows that, in conjunction with the catholicity of the local church's fellowship, there must be a catholicity of its mission. The entire local church is sent forth (*catholicity of the missionary subject*), i.e., by virtue of Baptism and the Eucharist, there is no one in the ecclesial community who is exempt from the missionary task. All the faithful, each one according to the charism received and the ministry exercised, around the ministry of the bishop and priests, the ministers of unity, are called to spread the Good News. The entire local church proclaims the entire Gospel: to the catholicity of the missionary subject is joined the *catholicity of the message*. The Gospel, which the Church proclaims, is not a doctrine, but a person, viz., Christ. Our mission calls for a full witness of him, without reductionisms that water down the message. No one may preach his own Gospel: all are asked to let themselves be continually evangelized by the Word of God so as to become faithful evangelizers of that Word.

By virtue of that Word, the local church must be critically aware of the culture surrounding it, a sign of contradiction, bringing to all human situations its preeminent hope (cf. 1 Pet 3:15). At the same time, it must be a traveling companion of the people to whom it proclaims the Word of God, so that the Gospel may be interlaced with the daily deeds of fraternity, where love becomes concrete and credible in the sharing of day-to-day life and in the choices taken on the side of the poor and the little ones of the earth. The catholicity of the message requires that the local church be able to say God's "no," but also "yes," in the many affirmations that people need in order to live and die well.

Finally, *the catholicity of the target audience of the Gospel* should be stressed: the entire local church proclaims the whole Gospel to the whole person, to every person. Openness to the Word and the Holy Spirit is not possible without, at the same time, openness to the full range of human needs and the target audience of the message. This is where it becomes imperative for every baptized person and the entire local church to commit themselves so that the preaching of the Good News will truly reach every person. In this way, there will be no area in the concrete fragment of history where the Word has not reached. Without this missionary urgency and passion, the catholicity of the local church grows feeble and dies: "An established Christianity in which all are Christians, but in a secret inner sanctum, no more resembles the Church Militant than the silence of death resembles the eloquence of passion" (Kierkegaard) (cf. LG 17).

3.3 The Communion of Churches

This emphatic affirmation of the priority of the local church in terms of communion and mission inevitably raises the question of the relationship between "local structure" and "universality" in the ecclesiology of communion. Does the priority of the local church mean that the universal Church doesn't exist? Or: How should we understand from this priority the idea of the Church's universality? How does it express itself in history?[5]

The answer to these questions is found in the fundamental thesis that the local church is the "Catholic Church" embodied in the concrete dimensions of space and time. The source from which an individual local church arises as fully church is the same mystery of the one Spirit and the one Christ, the one Word, the one Baptism and the one Bread, from which arises every other local church, these also being fully church. That is, the individual local church does not exhaust the possibilities of concrete embodiments of the "Catholic Church." In the same way, the individual Eucharistic Celebration – which also represents the entire mystery of the risen Lord – does not exhaust the possibilities of other Eucharistic Celebrations, equally full and authentic.

The individual local churches, therefore, are inter-related in fellowship, the foundation and manifestation of which is Eucharistic communion. "In ecclesiology, one plus one equals one: every local church manifests all the fullness of God's Church, because it is God's Church and not only part of it. There may be a plurality of manifestations of God's Church, but the Church remains one and the same, because it is always equal to itself [...]. The plurality of local churches does not destroy the unity of God's Church, just as the plurality of eucharistic gatherings does not destroy the unity of the Eucharist in time and space."[6]

The early Church lived this eucharistic dimension of fellowship intensely: the religious rite of the "leaven," a consecrated particle sent by the Roman bishop to the priests of the titular churches for the

Sunday celebration as a sign of Church unity; the letters of fellowship issued by the bishops to the faithful to attest their fellowship and to permit reception of the Eucharist at the churches visited; carrying the consecrated bread so as not to enter into fellowship with heretics in their territories; admission to the Eucharist and excommunication.[7] These are only a few signs of a widespread eucharistic perception of the Church and of fellowship among the local churches in the early centuries.

How is this unity of the churches, each one of which is the "Catholic Church" embodied in a definite place and time, expressed and nurtured historically?

In the local church the sign and minister of unity is the bishop. He represents Christ, the Head of the Church Body, in summoning the community to the banquet of the Lamb and proclaiming to that community the Word of the Lord (prophetic ministry), in offering the memorial of the sacrifice, and offering himself as a sacrifice through the transparency of his life (priestly ministry), in admitting people to eucharistic communion or excluding them from it — according to the Gospel mandate of binding and loosing — and in discerning and coordinating charisms in Church fellowship (pastoral ministry).

The bishop, who is assisted by the body of priests and deacons, is not outside the community, but in it and for it. He is not the exclusive repository of the Spirit, but the one who, because of his ministry of unity, has the charism of listening to and recognizing the Spirit, as he listens to and guides the Church (cf. LG 24-29).

Even as the unity of the local church has its highest expression in the Eucharistic Celebration presided over by the bishop, the unity of the local churches has its fullest historical manifestation in the reciprocal eucharistic reception of their bishops. Communicating in the Eucharist means, for them, to be recognized as heralds of the same Word, priests of the same sacrifice, pastors of the one and only People of God.

Communion in the Eucharist implies communion in the same faith, the same praise, the same mystery of unity. There is a very intense manifestation of eucharistic communion among the churches at the time of regional and ecumenical councils, when the bishops gather above all for a "celebration." The council is "celebrated": it has a liturgical-communional dimension. As J. D. Zizioulas writes:[8] "It seems that there was an intrinsic relationship between *conciliarity* and liturgical life in the early Church. Conciliar action should be noted originally, in many cases, in the context of the Eucharist; however, the purpose of that action seems to have been always that of leading the Church to sacramental unity. At the same time, an interrelation developed between conciliarity and the episcopate. In the early Church, and particularly at the time when only the bishop was head of the eucharistic congregation, this was probably one of the strongest reasons that led to the establishment of a strictly episcopal structure of conciliarity."

The ministers of unity of the local churches come together to meet one another and "welcome one another" in the one Eucharist, which each one of them presides over in his own church. From this lived, believed and celebrated unity, they also draw guidelines and answers for the life of their communities. Rooted in this experience is the ecclesiological view of "conciliarity." "The one Church must be seen as a conciliar community of local churches truly united in themselves. In this conciliar community, each local church possesses, in fellowship with the other local churches, the fullness of catholicity, bears witness to the same apostolic faith, and hence recognizes the other churches as belonging to the same Church of Christ and guided by the same Spirit[...]. They are united with each other, for they have received the same baptism and share in the same Eucharist; they recognize each other's members and ministers. They are one in their common mission of professing the Gospel of Christ by proclamation and service to the world."[9]

This conciliar dimension of the ecclesiology of fellowship is presented also in the teaching of Vatican II on the collegial union of the episcopacy: "Indeed, the very ancient practice whereby bishops duly established in all parts of the world were in communion with one another and with the Bishop of Rome in a bond of unity, charity and peace, and also the councils assembled together, in which more profound issues were settled in common, the opinion of the many having been prudently considered, both of these factors are already an indication of the collegiate character and aspect of the episcopal order; and the ecumenical councils held in the course of centuries are also manifest proof of that same character. And it is intimated also in the practice, introduced in ancient times, of summoning several bishops to take part in the elevation of the newly elected to the ministry of the high priesthood" (LG 22).

Within the college "each individual bishop represents his own church, but all of them together in union with the Pope represent the entire Church joined in the bond of peace, love and unity" (LG 23). While it affirms the primacy of the local church, the teaching of the college of bishops presents the Universal Church as the universal fellowship of churches, expressed and promoted by the ministry of unity of the episcopal college. Within this college or body and, therefore, in the fellowship of churches, from the earliest times there has been a ministry of unity. On the regional level, it is exercised by the archbishop or the patriarch, who, from the eucharistic standpoint, is the presiding minister of the Eucharist, which all the churches and all the bishops of that region partake of; on the level of the universal fellowship of churches, this ministry is carried out by the bishop of the church "which presides in love": the Church of Rome.

This universal ministry of unity among the churches, proper to the Bishop of Rome, is founded on the bond between the Roman Church and the martyrdom there of the Apostles Peter and Paul. "The communion of the witnesses of Peter and Paul has been as though entrusted to the local church of Rome, impressed on it, so that it may be the 'living remembrance' of that communion among all the churches."[10] The Vicar of Peter, having his See in the church of the martyrdom of Peter and Paul, presides above all over his church. But he is charged also with the ministry of communion among all the churches, both as their ultimate arbiter in the search for unity and as the promoter of fellowship through the word that "strengthens the brethren" (cf. Lk 22:32), the presiding ministry of the Eucharist, and concern for all the churches, to which he is committed, with the entire College of Bishops, to discern their own original charisms and coordinate them in fellowship.

This universal ministry of unity must never smother the life and growth of the local churches; rather, it must be at their service to help them overcome the conflicts that are always possible in history and develop in the fullness of the mystery of Christ. On the other hand, the local church is a true ecclesial subject and must be so in the regional and universal fellowship of the churches. It must neither be engulfed by that fellowship nor must it ever stand apart from it. A local church that pays no heed to fellowship with the other churches would contradict its own eucharistic and pneumatological nature, i.e., it would not faithfully profess the one Lord and the one Spirit, from whom it originated through the one Word, the one Baptism, and the one Bread. Therefore, a true appreciation of the autonomy and creativity of the local churches always goes hand in hand with a true appreciation of the collegial structures and the ministry of unity among the churches. In an effective collegial (or conciliar) life of the churches, conspicuous on the one hand are the dignity and originality proper to each local church and, on the other hand, the value and depth of catholic fellowship among the churches and in the individual local church.

Third Part

The Pilgrim Church:
Ecclesia Viatorum

Where Is the Church Heading?

With the Church's Trinitarian origin and its organization in the image of the Trinity (People of God and fellowship), Vatican II has rediscovered also the Trinitarian goal of the Church, her eschatological nature: the pilgrim people ("Ecclesia viatorum, in via et non in patria") travels toward the glory of the heavenly Jerusalem, an image and foreglimpse of which has been given to us in the figure of the Virgin Mary (cf. LG Chapters VII and VIII).

This eschatological character points up the provisional nature of all ecclesial realizations. *The Church has never "arrived."* On the contrary, the Church is by nature both poor and a servant, "semper renovanda et purificanda," "always in need of renewal and purification." She is not identified with the Kingdom; rather she is only its inchoate, initial form, the "Regnum revelatum, sed tectum cruce," the "Kingdom revealed, but hidden in the cross," the "Regnum praesens in mysterio," the Kingdom "present in mystery" (LG 3). In a healthy tension between the gift "already" received and the promise "not yet" completely fulfilled, the Church is growing toward the final manifestation of the Kingdom of God, fostered in the temporal pilgrimage by fellowship with the heavenly Church.

Within this tension, moreover, are the possibility and reality of sin in the Church — always a mystery of brokenness in our relationship with God and man — and the road to reconciliation as a re-acceptance of the gift of unity and a commitment to it, also among divided Christians. By virtue of its Trinitarian, communional and eschatological ecclesiology, Vatican Council II has opened new perspectives in ecumenical inquiry.

First of all, the Trinitarian origin of ecclesial fellowship indicates that the unity we seek is a gift from on high. Expressions of this conviction are the restoration of baptismal fellowship among divided Christians, and the commitment to the spiritual ecumenism of a change of heart in prayer and penance so as to be open to the gift of God (cf. LG 15 and UR 7 and 8).

Second, the communion of the Church "inter tempora" demands that we restore the elements which unite Catholic communion to the other Christian churches and ecclesial communities. The doctrine on the different degrees of communion in terms of the ontology of grace, as well as that on the "hierarchy of truths" in terms of the profession of faith, should be read in this light (cf. LG 15 and UR 11).

Finally, the eschatological nature of the People of God commits the Church to renew herself unceasingly by being open to the promise, common to all the faithful in Christ, so as to grow toward the unity he desires, as and when he desires it.

4. The Trinitarian Goal of the Church

4.1 The Eschatological Nature of the Pilgrim Church

Ecclesial communion, originating from on high, from the Father, through Christ, in the Spirit, and consisting in unity and the diversity of gifts and ministries in the image of Trinitarian communion, is not an end or goal in itself. It tends toward the origin from which it came and is a pilgrim on the way to the "heavenly homeland" (cf. Heb 11:14): "Ecclesia viatorum." In the Spirit and through Christ, it journeys toward the Father. It continually directs itself on high, toward the glory of the Lord of heaven and earth, which is also the complete fulfillment of each creature.

The eschatological dimension pervades and inspires the whole of Trinitarian ecclesiology, restored by Vatican II. Having sprung from God's initiating action and kindled ever anew by the memorial of the events of salvation, the Church is impelled by those events to open itself to the promised future; the gift "already" received is the foreglimpse and promise of a greater gift "not yet" completed. "The promised restoration which we are awaiting has already begun in Christ, is carried forward in the mission of the Holy Spirit, and through the Spirit continues in the Church, in which we learn through faith the meaning, too, of our temporal life, while we perform, with hope in the future the task committed to us in this world by the Father, and thus work out our salvation (cf. Phil 2:12)" (LG 48).

The gift received does not satisfy our expectations; it is a promise and beginning that overturns and changes those expectations, making them more alive and intense. The promised future thus becomes the quality of ecclesial being and action, the dimension that reaches and gives life to everything, and a reminder of the end, which gives meaning and value to every step of the way. From this state of tension between the "already" and the "not yet" three consequences result for the re-presentation and life of the Church.

First, the reminder of the heavenly homeland, "not yet" possessed, teaches the Church to *relativize itself.* She discovers that she is not an absolute but an instrument, not an end but a means, not a "sovereign body" but a poor and humble servant. She sees herself as on a journey, a People of God in exodus toward the promised land, in healthy tension toward complete fulfillment, which will come about "only in the glory of heaven when there will come the time of the restoration of all things (cf. Acts 3:21). At that time the human race as well as the entire world, which is intimately related to man and achieves its purpose through him, will be perfectly re-established in Christ (cf. Eph 1:10; Col 1:20; 2 Pet 3:10-13)" (LG 48).

In this condition of exodus, no acquisition or success must temper the ardor of expectancy in the Church. Any presumption of having arrived, any "ecstasy of fulfillment" should be seen as an illusion and betrayal. The Church is not the Kingdom of glory, but only the Kingdom begun, "praesens in mysterio," "present in mystery" (LG 3), "revelatum, su tectum cruce," "revealed but hidden in the cross" (Luther). It takes on the appearance of this passing world and dwells among creatures who groan and travail in pain until now and await the new heavens and the new earth (cf. LG 48).

Every identification of the Kingdom with the earth is to be rejected: the Church is "on the way and not in the homeland." Therefore, she is "always in need of being reformed," called to unceasing renewal and continual purification, unfulfilled and incapable of fulfillment by any human conquest. She knows that she does not possess the truth of her God but is as though possessed by it. And in the wonderment of praise, the toil of thought and the responsible preaching of the Word, she knows that she must let herself be increasingly possessed by her Spouse, to "move forward constantly toward the fullness of divine truth until the words of God reach their complete fulfillment in her" (*Dei Verbum* 8).

Nothing is farther from the style of a Church that is ever mindful of her heavenly homeland than an attitude of triumphalism, of giving in to the seduction of power and possession in this world. The People of God, born at the foot of the Cross and on a pilgrim journey through the long Good Friday of man's history, must never exchange the pale lights of any earthly glory for the light of the Glory promised at Easter. Against all the logic of this world, the ultimate goal of Christ's Church is to sing her *"Nunc dimittis,"* like the old Simeon, when there will rise, no longer veiled, the "light of the nations."

Second, the reminder of the "not yet" teaches the People of God, on a pilgrim journey in time, to relativize the grandeurs of this world. Everything is subject to the judgment of the Lord's promise. The presence of Christians in history is in the sign of exile and struggle: "Therefore, 'while we are at home in the body, we are away from the Lord' (2 Cor 5:6) and having the first-fruits of the Spirit we groan within ourselves (cf. Rom 8:23) and we desire to be with Christ (cf. Phil 1:23). By that same love, however, we are urged to live more for him, who died for us and rose again (cf. 2 Cor 5:15). We strive therefore to please God in all things (cf. 2 Cor 5:9) and put on the armor of God, that we may be able to stand against the wiles of the devil and resist in the evil day (cf. Eph 6:11-13)" (LG 48).

In the name of her goal and her greater hope, the Church will therefore have a counter-cultural and critical attitude toward all the shortsighted attainments of this world. Present in every human situation, at one with the poor and oppressed, it would be out of place for her to identify her hope with one of the hopes of history. But this does not signify noninvolvement on her part, or facile criticism: the vigilance required of the People of God is much more costly and demanding. It means taking on human hopes and at the same time evaluating them against the standard of the Lord's resurrection, which on the one hand sustains every authentic commitment to liberation and human advancement and, on the other hand, challenges any absolutizing of earthly goals.

In this double sense, the Church's hope, which is hope of the resurrection, is the resurrection of hope. It gives life to whatever is a prisoner of death and implacably shatters whatever claims to make itself an idol of life. Here is rooted the profound inspiration of the presence of Christians in different cultural, political and social contexts. In the name of her "eschatological reserve," the Church may not identify itself with any ideology, party force or system. But she must be a critical conscience for all people, a reminder of their origin and final goal, a stimulus so that among all people there may develop the whole person in every person.

The People of God, mindful of the heavenly homeland, feels unsettled and restless. It is a free people because of faith and a servant because of love. This is not a Church of the establishment, of compromise or spiritual noninvolvement. The goal which makes Christians both foreigners and pilgrims in this world is not a dream that removes them from reality, but a stimulating and critical force of commitment for justice and peace in the world of today (cf. Chapter IV of *Gaudium et Spes,* on the Church's mission in the contemporary world).

Finally, the reminder of the heavenly homeland, "already" presaged both in promise and in gift, fills the Church with hope and joy. "Reckoning, therefore, that 'the sufferings of this present time are not worth comparing with the glory that is to be revealed in us' (Rom 8:18; cf. 2 Tim 2:11-12), strong in faith we look for 'the blessed hope, the appearing of the glory of our great God and Savior, Jesus Christ' (Tit 2:13)" (LG 48).

Despite the trials and contradictions of the present, the People of God already exults in the hope which God's promise has enkindled in it. In the Virgin Mary it already contemplates its life course and the final triumph of grace in it. Mary, who "stands out in eminent and singular fashion" as a member of the Church, is an "exemplar" of the Church community, a virgin and mother. Even as she, "by her belief and obedience, not knowing man but overshadowed by the Holy Spirit...brought forth on earth the Father's Son" (LG 63), so the Church "faithfully fulfilling the Father's will, by receiving the word of God in faith becomes herself a mother. By her preaching she brings forth to a new and immortal life the children who are born to her in Baptism, conceived of the Holy Spirit and born of God. [The Church] herself is a virgin, who keeps the faith given to her by her Spouse whole and entire" (LG 64).

With Mary, who has "advanced in her pilgrimage of faith, and faithfully persevered in her union with her Son unto the cross" (LG 58), the pilgrim Church in faith and hope raises her song of praise to the Lord, because of the great things that he is now doing for her (cf. Lk 1:46 ff.). At the same time, in the communion of "saints" in Christ, Mary "cares for the brethren of her Son, who still journey on earth surrounded by dangers and difficulties, until they are led into the happiness of their true home" (LG 62).

This union of the pilgrim Church with the heavenly Church, founded in the one Lord and the one Spirit, is a source of strength and joy for the People of God. "Until the Lord comes in his majesty, and all the angels with him [...] some of his disciples are exiles on earth, some having died are being purified, and others are in glory, beholding 'clearly God himself triune and one, as he is.' But all in various ways and degrees are in communion in the same love for God and neighbor, and all sing the same hymn of glory to our God. For all who are in Christ, having his Spirit, form one Church and cleave together in him (cf. Eph 4:16)" (LG 49).

In this communion, stronger than death because it is founded on the resurrected Lord, there is a true exchanging of spiritual goods, wherein our weakness is helped by the fraternal interest of "those in heaven" (cf. LG 49). Sustained by the hope which guarantees that the last words of history will not be pain, sin or death, but joy, grace and life, the Church is like the pilgrims of Jerusalem on the road to their journey's end, already exulting over it: "I was glad when they said to me, 'Let us go to the house of the Lord!' " (Ps 122:1).

The Church's joy does not rise from the presumption that she is building with her own hands a ladder up to heaven, a new tower of Babel in a self-imprisoned world. Her peace and her power are firmly planted in her eschatological nature, i.e., in the certainty that the Spirit of the living God is already at work in time upon earth, building up the future promised by God. God has "time" for his people and with them builds his dwelling: Jerusalem, longed for and expected, is coming down out of heaven (cf. Rv 21:2). The faithful are left with the task of living the mystery of Advent in the heart of human events: "The Spirit and the Bride say, 'Come!' " To them the God of life answers: "Surely I am coming soon!" (Rv 22:17, 20). Rediscovery of the Trinitarian origin, form and goal of the Church causes the engaging and joyful message of the "good news" to resound in a new way in ecclesiology.

4.2   On the Way to a Fuller Unity

In the tension between the origin and heavenly homeland, between the "already" and the "not yet," we note the possibility and reality of sin in the

Church: "Just as Christ carried out the work of redemption in poverty and under persecution, so the Church is called to follow the same path that it might communicate to people the fruits of salvation [...]. While Christ, 'holy, innocent, and undefiled' (Heb 7:26), knew nothing of sin (cf. 2 Cor 5:21), but came to expiate only the sins of the people (cf. Heb 2:17), the Church, embracing sinners in her bosom, is at the same time holy and always in need of being purified, and incessantly pursues the way of penance and renewal" (LG 8).

If by virtue of her Trinitarian foundation and the permanent action of the Holy Spirit the Church is "indefectibly holy" (LG 39), i.e., holy on the level of the ontology of grace because she is sanctified by Christ and by his Spirit, yet, sin is not thereby excluded in the Church. Holiness *of* the Church is not identified with holiness *in* the Church. The task of the baptized is therefore to become with their entire life that which they became with Baptism. In the baptism of faith they truly become children of God and sharers in the divine nature. In this way they are really made holy. Then, too, by God's gift, they must hold on to and complete in their lives this holiness which they have received" (LG 40).

When this does not take place, the reality of sin appears. It is a mystery of our separation from God and from one another, an alienation from the divine plan of unity, a source of isolation and division within the womb of ecclesial communion. The Church is thus "at the same time holy and sinful": holy in the

Trinitarian depth of her mystery; sinful and in need of conversion and reform in her historical events. In this light we are to understand also the reality of the division that painfully exists among the baptized. It should not be confused with the variety raised up by the Spirit and always needed for the growth of the Body, nor can it be imputed to sin in the person born already in separation. Nevertheless, it calls attention to the "mystery of iniquity" as its ultimate root and requires a path of reconciliation, as a new acceptance of the gift of unity and a commitment to the historical realization of that unity (cf. *Unitatis Redintegratio*, n. 1)

Trinitarian ecclesiology, which tends to express the icon of the Trinity in the present and in the future of the Church, cannot be other than "ecumenical," i.e., committed to overcoming divisions in order to build up unity in the variety that the Lord wills. Not without reason are the following words — a beautiful compendium of the Church's Trinitarian perspective — found at the beginning of the conciliar decree on ecumenism. "This is the sacred mystery of the unity of the Church, in Christ and through Christ, with the Holy Spirit energizing its various functions. It is a mystery that finds its highest exemplar and source in the unity of the Persons of the Trinity: of one God, the Father and the Son in the Holy Spirit, one God" (UR 2).

What prospects does the Trinitarian ecclesiology of Vatican Council II offer to the ecumenical search for unity? What pathways does it point to for avoiding sin, which lies at the heart of every division, and hence, for fully realizing the divine plan of unity? By analogy to what takes place in the fellowship already given and existing historically through Christ and in the Spirit, the unity to be sought should be seen in relation to its origin, its form and its final Trinitarian goal.

First of all, the Trinitarian origin of ecclesial union makes it clear that the unity sought by the ecumenical movement is a gift from on high. Therefore, it should first be recognized where it is already present and accepted where it is not yet present. Recognition of the unity already existing is expressed especially in the profession of baptismal communion. Those "who believe in Christ and have been truly baptized are in communion with the Catholic Church even though this communion is imperfect [...]. All those who have been justified through Baptism are members of Christ's body and have a right to be called Christian, and so are correctly accepted as brethren by the children of the Catholic Church" (UR 3; cf. UR 22).

It is not only Baptism, however, which unites divided Christians: "Some and even very many, of the significant elements and endowments which together go to build up and give life to the Church herself can exist outside the visible boundaries of the Catholic Church: the written Word of God; the life of grace; faith, hope and charity, along with the other interior gifts of the Holy Spirit, and visible elements, too. All of these, which come from Christ and lead back to Christ,·belong by right to the one Church of

Christ [...]. These separated churches and communities as such, though we believe them to be deficient in some respects, have by no means been deprived of significance and importance in the mystery of salvation..." (UR 3; cf. UR 22 on the Lord's Supper).

The logic of the "return to the one flock" identified with the Roman Catholic Church, proper to visibilist ecclesiology, is here surmounted. Restoration of the Trinitarian origin of ecclesial communion and, hence, of the primacy of God's initiating action helps us recognize God's work with new freedom, beyond the visible limits of what was considered to be the "perfect society" ("societas perfecta").

In addition to the unity already present, because it has been given from on high, there is need to welcome the gift to overcome disunity. We must open ourselves in adoration and penance to God's work. "There can be no ecumenism worthy of the name without a change of heart. For it is from renewal of the inner life of our minds (cf. Eph 4:23), from self-denial and unstinted love, that yearnings for unity take their rise and develop in a mature way. We should therefore pray to the Holy Spirit for the grace to be genuinely self-denying, humble, gentle in the service of others, and to have an attitude of fraternal generosity toward them" (UR 7).

"This change of heart and holiness of life, along with public and private prayer for the unity of Christians, should be regarded as the soul of the entire ecumenical movement, and merits the name 'spiritual ecumenism' " (UR 8). Trinitarian ecclesiology gives the strongest theological motivation for this ecumenism of holiness and invocation. If unity comes from on high, "from the Trinity," it can be received only in an adoring and responsive openness to the mystery of the Father, through the Son, in the experience of the Holy Spirit. Only from the Trinity comes the oneness that we are seeking!

Second, the Trinitarian form of ecclesiastical communion shows that the unity sought from ecumenism should not be understood as barren uniformity, but as unity in diversity, communion in variety. The fullness of the mystery, which is the Church, her "catholicity," is completely embodied in the local church. The universal Church, a communion of local churches, each one of which is fully Church, is therefore one in diversity, communion in Christ and in the Spirit in a variety of local embodiments. The same catholic communion of churches, however, does not rule out the possibility that the Church can be embodied also in other local churches, which are not in historical communion with Rome. Rising above the visibilist identification between the Church as Body of Christ and the Roman Catholic Church, Vatican II states that "the one Church of Christ which in the Creed is professed as one, holy, catholic and apostolic [...] *subsists* [author's emphasis] in the Catholic Church" (LG 8).

The verb *"subsistit,"* ("subsists") corrects the *"est"* ("is") of the original text, recognizing the fullness of ecclesial reality in the Catholic Church, but without excluding the possible embodiment of the Church in other Christian communities. On this is based the conciliar teaching of the "degrees of communion," which, in abandoning the logic of the "all or nothing" (the Catholic Church is *the* Church, the other Christian communities are *not*), recognizes the embodiment of the ecclesial mystery in different degrees in the various Christian communities, depending on the elements of ecclesiality (Word of God, sacraments, ordained ministry, and so forth) present in them (cf. LG 15). Thus, when all the essential elements are recognized (as in the Eastern churches, for example), we speak of "churches." On the other hand, we use the expression "ecclesial communities" when recognition of ecclesial communion is not as full (cf. UR 1, 3, 4).

But what elements are truly essential in order to have the presence of the "Catholic Church"? The teaching of the "hierarchy of truths," according to which "there exists an order or 'hierarchy' of truths, since they vary in their relation to the fundamental Christian faith" (UR 11), makes it possible not to absolutize what is relative in the profession of faith. The distinction between apostolic tradition in the Church and the succession of the apostolic ministry,[1] which prevents any simple identification of one with the other, enables us to recognize continuity with the Apostles and their preaching even when there is no ministerial apostolic succession.[2]

The reference to the communion of the undivided Church of the early centuries reveals that it is not appropriate to require for re-establishment of unity more than what was required at that time for maintaining it. The ecclesiology of communion thus opens possibilities for reciprocal acceptance among the churches and ecclesial communities — something unthinkable in the visibilistic and legalistic conception of the past. The form of unity that results from this gradual process of mutual acceptance appears as a conciliar communion of local churches truly united among themselves. That communion is rooted in the one Spirit, the one Word, the one Baptism and the one Bread, in the ministry that is mutually recognized.[3]

While objective differences and difficulties are not to be overlooked, it is evident that the road to a fuller unity is possible. It is linked to the commitment of each church to be more fully Church, above all locally, and to be willing to seek together with the other churches the most suitable historical expressions of the unity already existing, so as to grow toward the unity not yet fulfilled. The more the local churches become an icon of the Trinity, all the more will they become united in praise of the one Trinitarian God, so that the world may believe! (cf. Jn 17:21)

Lastly, the eschatological journey's end of the People of God shows that the unity sought by the ecumenical movement for reconciliation of separated Christians, calls for a constant openness to the promise, so that the Lord's words "that all may be one" will be fulfilled, when and as he wills. In this sense, ecumenism is a perennial reminder of the temporary nature of the churches and their need for continual change and reform and, at the same time, of the hope which Christians are called to explain before the world (cf. 1 Pet 3:15). A search for unity and a missionary openness of the People of God to all the nations meet here. The Church, coming from Trinitarian unity, tends to return to it, achieving the unity of the human race. To that end, she is more strongly aware of the need and passion for unity, which will overcome the stumbling block of the preaching of a divided Gospel.

The promised future becomes a restlessness and a stimulus to seeking unity, so we may proclaim it believably and build it up in history. "In this way the Church both prays and labors in order that the entire world may become the People of God, the Body of the Lord and the Temple of the Holy Spirit, and that in Christ, the Head of all, all honor and glory may be rendered to the Creator and Father of the universe" (LG 17). Perennial reform and missionary zeal are aspects of the same longing for the Trinity, from which the Church comes and toward which she advances in her journey through time.

Notes

Chapter 1

1. Yves Congar accepts — not without due reserve — the expression used time and again by N. A. Nissiotis: *Pneumatologie ou 'Christomonisme' dans la tradition latine?* in Ephemerides Theologicae Lovanienses 45 (1969), 394-416. Cf. N. A. Nissiotis, *La pneumatologie ecclésiologique au service de l'unité de l'Eglise*, in *Istina* 14 (1967), 323-340.

2. R. Bellarmino, *De controversiis Christianae fidei adversus nostri temporis haereticos*, vol. II: *Prima Controversia generalis*, book III: *De Ecclesia militante*, chap. II: *De definitione Ecclesiae*, Ingolstadt 12601, 137-138.

3. Cf., for instance, O. Dibelius, *Das Jahrhundert der Kirche*, Berlin 1926: perhaps the first one to use the expression.

4. Yves Congar, *Chronique de trente ans d'études ecclésiologiques*, in *Sainte Eglise, études et approches ecclésiologiques*, Paris 1963, 514. Cf. the entire text: 445-696 and — on the history of the Church — by the same author, *L'église de Saint Augustin à l'époque moderne*, Paris 1970.

5. Yves Congar, *Chronique...*, *op. cit.*, 450.

6. Cf. the work of E. Mersch, *Le corps Mystique du Christ. Etudes de Théologie historique*, Paris-Brussels 1936, 2 vols.; idem, *La Théologie du Corps mystique*, 2 vols., Paris 1944.

7. Intervention of Card. L. J. Suenens at the 33rd General Congregation, December 4, 1962: *Acta Synodalia* I, IV, 223.

8. Intervention of Card. G. B. Montini: *Acta Synodalia*, I, IV, 292.

9. Cf. the text of the draft declaration: *Acta Synodalia* I, IV, 12-121.

10. The expression, from St. Cyprian in his *De Oratione Dominica* 23: PL 4, 553, is quoted in LG 4.

11. *Baptism, Eucharist and Ministry,* Faith and Order Paper N. 111, Geneva: World Council of Churches, 1982; *Eucharist,* n. 5.

12. For a detailed analysis of this text from *Lumen Gentium,* cf. B. Forte, *The Church in the Eucharist, a study in eucharistic ecclesiology in the light of Vatican II,* Naples 1975, 210.

13. E. Zoghby, *Unità e diversità della Chiesa,* in *La Chiesa del Vaticano II,* edited by G. Barauna, Florence 1967, 522.

14. G. Philips, *La Chiesa e il suo mistero nel Concilio Vaticano II,* Milan 1969, vol. I, 87.

15. *Il mistero della Chiesa e dell'Eucaristia alla luce del mistero della Santa Trinità,* Document by Monaco on Catholic-Orthodox dialogue, 1982, I, 6.

16. St. Augustine, *De Civitate Dei,* XVIII, 51, 2: PL 41, 614, quoted in LG 8.

Chapter 2

1. Pius X, encyclical *Vehementer Nos,* February 11, 1906: ASS 39 (1906), 8-9.

2. In *Theologische Quartalschrift* 1823, 497: the context is that of a critical essay on the legalistic and naturalistic idea of the Church proper to theologians of the Enlightenment.

3. Cf. Y. Congar, *Ministeri e comunione ecclesiale,* Bologna 1973, 12.

4. C. Moeller, *Storia della struttura e delle idee della LG,* in *La teologia dopo il Vaticano II,* edited by J. M. Miller, Brescia 1967, 159. There was no dearth of resistance, and it emerged in the final result: cf. A. Acerbi, *Due ecclesiologie. Ecclesiologia giuridica e ecclesiologia di comunione nella LG,* Bologna 1975.

5. *Relatio* of Bishop G. Garrone at the 82nd General Congregation, on September 17, 1964: *Acta Synodalia* III, I, 500-501.

6. Y. Congar, *La chiesa come popolo di Dio,* in *Concilium* I (1965), 19-20.

7. Cf. *Acta Synodalia* II, III, 382-384 (intervention of Bishop A. Charue).

8. Allocution *Magnificate Dominum* of November 2, 1954 to the cardinals and bishops. The text of *Mediator Dei,* AAS 39 (1947) 553, though mentioned by LG 10 in a footnote, does not actually contain the formula.

9. *Baptism, Eucharist and Ministry,* op. cit., *Ministry,* n. 8.

10. Cf. Y. Congar, *Ministeri e comunione ecclesiale, op. cit.,* 18ff.

11. U. Benedetti, *L'interpretazione della laicità,* in Aa.Vv., *Laicità nella chiesa,* Milan 1977, 1982.

12. W. Kasper, *Il mondo come luogo del vangelo*, in Id., *Fede e storia*, Brescia, 1975, 160.

13. Refer to the text in Gratian's *Decretum* (around 1140) on the "two types of Christians": C. 7. C.XII, q. I: Friedberg I. Leipzig 1879, 678.

Chapter 3

1. Cf. P. Nautin, *Je crois à l'Esprit Saint dans la Sainte Eglise pour la Résurrection de la chair. Etude sur l'histoire et la theologie du Symbole*, Paris 1947.

2. *Baptism, Eucharist and Ministry*, op. cit., *Eucharist*, n. 19.

3. *Confessio Augustana* (1530): VII, *De Ecclesia*.

4. On this text cf. B. Forte, *La chiesa nell'eucaristia. Per un'ecclesiologia eucaristica alla luce del Vaticano II*, Naples 1975, 238ff.

5. Cf. J. Zizioulas, *L'être écclesial*, Geneva 1981, 187ff.

6. N. Afanassieff, *La chiesa che presiede nell'amore*, in Aa.Vv., *Il primato di Pietro*, Bologna 1965, 510-511.

7. Cf. L. Hertling, *Communio. Chiesa e Papato nell'antichità cristiana*, Rome 1961; and W. Elert, *Abendmahl und Kirchengemeinschaft in der alten Kirche, hauptsachlich des Ostens*, Berlin 1954.

8. J. D. Zizioulas, *The Development of Conciliar Structures to the Time of the First Ecumenical Councils*, in *Councils and the Ecumenical Movement*, World Council Studies 5, Geneva 1968, 51.

9. *Breaking Barriers. Nairobi 1975*. The Official Report of the Fifth Assembly of the WCC, London 1976, Section II: *What Unity Requires*, n. 3, 60.

10. J. M. Tillard, *L'éveque de Rome*, Paris 1982, 153; cf. also B. Forte, *Il primato nell'eucaristia*, in *Asprenas* 23 (1976) 391-410, and J. J. v. Allmen, *La primauté de l'Eglise de Pierre et de Paul*, Paris – Fribourg 1977.

Chapter 4

1. *Baptism, Eucharist, Ministry*, op. cit., *Ministry*, nn. 34-35.

2. Cf. B. Forte, *Verso un consenso ecumenico sul ministero ordinato?*, in *Asprenas* 28 (1981) 155-174.

3. Cf. the text of Section II, n. 3, of the Assembly of the World Council in Nairobi (1975): *Breaking Barriers. Nairobi 1975*, London 1976, 60.

SP **St. Paul Book & Media Centers:**

Alexandria, VA
Anchorage, AK
Boston, MA
Charleston, SC
Chicago, IL
Cleveland, OH
Dedham, MA
Edison, NJ
Honolulu, HI
Los Angeles, CA
Miami, FL
New Orleans, LA
New York, NY
King of Prussia, PA
San Antonio, TX
San Diego, CA
San Francisco, CA
St. Louis, MO
Staten Island, NY
Toronto, Ontario, CANADA